BEING FLAWESOME

BEING FLAWESOME

Becoming Perfect, the Journey of Transformation

NICHOLAS MATTHEWS
Foreword by Bill Brown

RESOURCE *Publications* • Eugene, Oregon

BEING FLAWESOME
Becoming Perfect, the Journey of Transformation

Copyright © 2020 Nicholas Matthews. All rights reserved. Except for brief quotations in critical publications or reviews, no part of this book may be reproduced in any manner without prior written permission from the publisher. Write: Permissions, Wipf and Stock Publishers, 199 W. 8th Ave., Suite 3, Eugene, OR 97401.

Resource Publications
An Imprint of Wipf and Stock Publishers
199 W. 8th Ave., Suite 3
Eugene, OR 97401

www.wipfandstock.com

PAPERBACK ISBN: 978-1-7252-8834-8
HARDCOVER ISBN: 978-1-7252-8835-5
EBOOK ISBN: 978-1-7252-8836-2

12/21/20

To the flawed becoming flawesome
The flawesome becoming perfected.

To the curious
The student and the accomplished.

To whom know their identity and to whom still searching
For the confident in character and those exploring.

To the seen. The known. The heard. The validated. The loved. The needed
For those still discovering.

To Sarah, Daniel, and Joseph. Liz and John.
To the teachers, lecturers, and companions who have taught me, shaped me, and journeyed with me.

Bill Brown—for your passion and enthusiasm
Tin Tran—for shared dreams and inspiration
Sarah Cumming—for your kind words

With special gratitude to Wipf & Stock Publishers.

To all on this journey of becoming perfected.

The Lord bless you
and keep you.

Contents

Foreword by Bill Brown		ix
Defining Principles		xi
1	The Human Race: A Brief Introduction	1
2	Being Flawesome	7
3	All Stories Have a Beginning	9
4	Encounters with Doubt	13
5	Being Perfect	17
6	Pursuing Perfection and the Journey of Discipleship	22
7	Recognizing and Making Jesus Lord	25
8	Comparison	31
9	Falling Upwards	42
10	The Challenge of Identity: The Front Line in the Battle of the Mind	48
11	Identifying the High Ground	50
12	Of Idols and Icons	52
13	Perfect	65
14	The Validating God	70
15	The Importance of Names	72
16	How God Validates	86
17	The Journey of Discipleship is a Journey of Movement	92
18	Being Perfect	97
19	The Battle for Identity	100
20	Defining Identity	103

21	The Human Condition	105
22	I Am Who I Am	109
23	The World Awaits your Identity	115
24	To Be a Human?	118
25	Living Inside a Human Body	120
26	What Makes us Human?	123
27	Created for Community	129
28	Became. Becoming. Become.	146
29	Progressive Salvation	147
30	Discipleship's Role in Freedom	149
31	The Secret Life of Humans	153
32	Lessons from the Lives of Ancient Kings	157
33	The Role of the Idol	160
34	Following Jesus is Experienced Mainly Through our Minds	177
35	Confidence in the Name of Jesus	187
36	Practicing the Greatest Act of Defiance	190
	Also Available from the Author	197
	Reader Reviews	201
	Bibliography	205

Foreword

'Being Flawesome' aroused and piqued my curiosity from the moment I saw the title. What does it mean? From the first page to the last, I found myself engaged in the vulnerable and transparent conversation into which Nik Matthews invites readers about why we settle for less than the 'life to the full' that Jesus came to give. The capacity to live out our identity as children of God is influenced significantly by the hundreds of choices we make every day, and the choices we make today determine the stories we tell or are told about us tomorrow.

The fact that every human being bears the image of God, the fact that God has placed eternity in every heart stirs up within us the taste for life as she was meant to be lived. But then there are the inevitable questions and doubts that surface that distract us and tend to eat away at our confidence and distance us from what God offers us. Throughout the book, Nik is honest about the doubts and decisions we all face and urges us not to park with the doubts but to embrace the life offered by Jesus and enabled by the Spirit having the run of our lives.

Are there signposts, guard rails, wisdom guidelines, and models of how to navigate the seasons of life and issues and doubts that confront us from day—to—day? The way Nik grounds the conversation in normal everyday language and with many real-life examples, both his own and those of others, with which people can readily identify and relate makes the book accessible, and I found myself wanting to turn the page to see how different scenarios would be explored and understood. Questions of our value and purpose, the needs of seeing and being seen, knowing and being known, loving and being loved, were not shirked, ignored or by-passed but wrestled with and considered in light of Scripture and ultimately in the light of the life, death, and resurrection of Jesus.

In becoming a human being and moving into our neighborhood, Jesus modeled out how to live in a vital and intimate relationship with God, his Father. His default position, in contrast to that of all humanity, was 'Not my will, but yours be done.' The only thing that we have recorded that Jesus's followers asked him to teach them was how to pray, and that prayer has as a central piece, 'Your will be done.' The fact that he was tempted in every way like we are gives us great confidence that he has the resources to help us in our time of need. Jesus' death and the victory shout of 'It is finished!' declared loudly and clearly that the sin and guilt that robs us of the capacity to embrace life has been dealt with decisively. Satan is a defeated but a desperate foe. Jesus' resurrection demonstrated that death has lost its sting, and forever Jesus is alive. He wants to live his life in and through us by his Spirit, the same Spirit that raised Jesus from the dead.

This is a hope-filled book that guides us in being totally alive to God and dead to sin. It offers insights that help set us to be free to live and love and respond as representatives of Jesus and to partner with Jesus in his mission. This is a book that provides keys to embrace every day as a gift and live it well by factoring Jesus into every decision we make, allowing our minds to be renewed by taking captive every thought to make it obedient to Christ. Do yourself, and those around you, a favor by savouring the opportunity for a life-changing adventure.

What a privilege to have read Nik's manuscript. I have found it both engaging and provoking, and what a great gift he has offered to his readers.

Rev. Dr. Bill Brown
Pastor Emeritus Syndal Baptist Church and Pastoral Coach,
Baptist Union of Victoria
Former Chair of Australian Baptist Ministries

Defining Principles

Twelve principles define the foundation of this book. I choose to present these principles in a non-prescriptive manner, nor a how-to guide. Instead, they underpin the narrative and guiding philosophy contained within, equipping the reader to engage with these principles through the book's dialogue.

The Twelve Principles:

- Principle 1: God is the definition of perfection, referred to within the Bible as being Awesome. We are perfected through Jesus while being perfected through the work of the Holy Spirit
- Principle 2: Our ancestors rejected perfect living in Eden and initiated a fractured and flawed existence. We now navigate this reality
- Principle 3: We experience temptation through perceived deficiency. However, there is no lack, nor deficiency, within the Kingdom of God
- Principle 4: We act from a position of deficiency when we allow doubt to influence our lives
- Principle 5: God is a validating God, and we crave validation; to be seen, to be heard, to be known, to be loved, and to be needed
- Principle 6: God offers life in its fullest, while the Devil lies, kills, steals, and destroys
- Principle 7: The Devil will aggravate, highlight, and promote our flaws
- Principle 8: God calls us to participate in the transformational journey of discipleship

- Principle 9: We are responsible, through the Holy Spirit, for the renewing of our minds and the transformation of our lives
- Principle 10: Tension exists between what we are and who we are
- Principle 11: We can wrongly assume our flawed character defines our identity
- Principle 12: Our identity is found within, and liberated through, the name of Jesus

1

The Human Race: A Brief Introduction

God never forces a person's will into surrender, and He never begs.
—Oswald Chambers[1]

THE CURTAIN TO OUR history begins with the story of Genesis. A tale transporting us to the origin of the human race. To the place where we discover our hope, and we learn of our struggle.

Partway through the narrative, we're provided with an intimate and friendly glimpse of God walking the land:

> And they heard the sound of the LORD God walking in the garden in the cool of the day.[2]

The scene follows the fall of Adam and Eve. Although it requires a level of speculation to conclude this "walking in the cool of the day" was a regular occurrence, it would seem rather odd and somewhat unlikely that God would commence this affectionate habit after the fall; after a barrier is placed between God and humans. I do consider, with some level of personal conviction, that this "walking in the cool of the day" would have been a daily habit between God and humans. It is this daily habit that provides clarity as to God's desire for a relationship with us.

---

1. Chambers, *Utmost for His Highest*
2. Gen 3:8, ESV

Unfortunately, the human rebellion broke this intimate communion. We chose to wander from this good life, this perfect life, and by doing so, we entered the darkness of the unknown. We turned from God, and we took matters into our own hands, and we discovered what it means to suffer the consequences of our actions and of internalizing our freewill.

Satan had offered temptation as a means to investigate his kingdom of dirt, and we reciprocated by choosing to wallow in the mud.

There is much we have learned about the human body, and there remains much to be discovered. We are daily advancing our knowledge of the human frame while gaining great insight as to the intricate working of the mind. We're identifying new physical malfunctions and understanding new psychological triggers for dysfunction. Yet, for many, mystery still shrouds our spiritual life.

Through this book, I aim to explore the relationship between the functioning of the physical and the spiritual. We are continuing to learn how to live inside a human body.

I do consider it as being highly conceivable that upon turning away from God, God's love receded from the center of the human soul as humanity sought alternative sources of fulfillment. As God's love receded, a void, an emptiness, at the center of the human soul formed, a self-imposed vacuum realized through our self-declaration of independence. Today, we continue to be impacted by this inherited reality, and we can feel and perceive the tangible void this emptiness generates.

Upon realizing we do not have the capacity within ourselves to fill this void, we pursue and turn towards alternatives. Temptation offers a broad array of enticing options, and the success of temptation is that it works; albeit, only in the temporary. Yet, the temptation may only require a brief window of opportunity to create the shame and guilt that will hijack our ability to reach out for help; while, in some cases, for addiction to take hold.

For many people, the thrill of engaging with temptation does provide a false sense of having felt needs met through instant gratification. And if temptation achieves this, it can then gain precious extended time to become lodged. The lure soon opens the door for an idol to enter between cracks in our foundation and take up residence in the heart of our life. Or, as discussed later, to become lodged on the high ground of our life, the place reserved for Jesus.

God created us for a covenantal relationship, and to realize this at the human level, he created our bodies in such a unique manner that his love could reside at the center of our lives, at the center of our very being. While being accurate that we can function without God's love in our lives, billions do, we cannot truly live without God's love at the center of what makes a human a human. Being void of God's love, we painstakingly continue our natural and driven search for ways to alleviate this love deficit. A quest that can be agonizing and lead to many heartaches, many relationships strained, and much experimentation with product and experience to nullify the devastating impact resulting from this deficit of love.

God's love belongs at the very center of our lives; it's our birthright. And God's love needs to be present at the most rooted foundation of human identity.

The moment God's love enters our lives, it flows to the innermost place, unable to go further because it has reached the depths.[3] Confidence and assurance in this reality will allow God's love to be expressed externally to family, friends, and the community far and wide. Similar to the pay-it-forward expression, a philosophy rooted in ancient Greek tradition and popularized by Hammond[4]. The simplest re-telling of this concept is the love passed between generations; a mother loves her daughter, who, in turn, loves her daughter with this same love. The same with God; God loves us so we can love others.

Void of God's love (or rather, being unsure of God's love), we painfully become exposed to the human manufactured experience of a deficit and begin to internalize our search and need for love (and with it, acceptance and purpose). We gaze internally, discover a vacuum, and become self-focused on the desperate need for our remedy. This search for a solution can become a self-centric living, selfish living, and, to the more extreme, narcissistic and hedonistic. For the married couple, lasting love will only work if there is a clearly defined and identified channel for love to be externalized. Focusing on the self is not wrong; in fact, we do need to investigate our inner lives to follow Jesus as a disciple fully. And by doing so, we learn how to live within the human body.

The challenge for humans is when we invite idols and destructive elements into the sacredness of the center of our lives, and then, resulting from impulsive habits, we empower these idols to form and germinate through all areas of our being. And this is why addiction is problematic.

The impulse to fill a need through gambling on an eventuality where we are powerless to determine the outcome has the potential to impact not only our financial health; but our emotions, our sense of value, our psychological disposition, our families, and our relationships. When this is the case, the addiction to gambling has taken up residence within this love deficit, and when left unattended, will grow not only through the physical, but

---

3. Refer to Rom 8:38–39 NIV
4. Hammond, *Garden of Delight*

also through the emotional and the spiritual cavities of the gambler's life. We are integrated people without the ability to control the knock-on effects from one area of our lives to the next.

As with the Titanic, the bulk-heads from one compartment to the next are not complete, and the rising water renders the allegorical ship in a state of distress. "There is nothing like a collision at sea to ruin your day," was a plaque hanging in a ship's wheelhouse my wife and I once worked on. Light-hearted in fair weather, yes, but a dire prophecy to keep the watchkeeper in a state of high alert while traversing crowded shipping lanes in fading light with only rough seas and strong coffee to accompany them through the long hours of the midnight watch.

I use the example of gambling and addiction for ease in its comprehension, but we may use many other cases. Any instance that renders us vulnerable.

While it remains true, we can discover new depths and expressions of God's love; God's love goes no deeper than the extent it has already penetrated the precise moment we invite God into our lives. God's love becomes all-sufficient the moment we start following Jesus.

Our understanding of this love and our level of liberation within this love will deepen as we mature, and to be experienced through our ongoing journey of discovering the fullness of God's love. The book of Ephesians gives credence to the fullness of this provision:

> And I pray that you, being rooted and established in love, may have power, together with all the Lord's holy people, to grasp how wide and long and high and deep is the love of Christ.[5]

While the book of Romans sheds undeniable light on the all-encompassing and everlasting nature of the love relationship between God and humans:

> If God is for us, who can be against us?... Who shall separate us from the love of Christ? Shall trouble or hardship or persecution or famine or nakedness or danger or sword?... No, in all these things we are more than conquerors through him who loved us. For I am convinced that neither death nor life, neither angels nor demons, neither the present nor the future, nor any powers, neither height nor depth, nor anything else in all creation, will be able to separate us from the love of God that is in Christ Jesus our Lord.[6]

---

5. Eph 3:17–19, NIV
6. Rom 8:31–39 NIV abridged

Whereas Paul goes somewhat into detail in the above passages, the anchor verse found in Genesis recalls that upon pondering humanity, God spoke that we are *"very good."*[7] Simply put, this is the basis on which our identity needs to rest. We are *"very good"*: the first validation as given to the human species, and this now provides us with precedence to the proper use of validation. Validation outside of love can lead to a terrible result to the recipient, and the importance of God's perfect validation is discussed through this book.

God's love as being the foundation of our lives means there is no deficit, and really, the only direction God's love can go is out, as it cannot go any deeper.

Thankfully, our ancestors did return to God, but the relationship was to be most different. God no longer walked on the earth in communion with us, and he needed to display his character and his ways through a portable tabernacle.[8] It seems ludicrous to consider that the creator of everything, the sun, the moon, the stars, and people, would be confined to reside within a box. We did this to God. Complex rules and regulations needed to be engaged to meet with God in this new inhibitive dwelling place.[9] Not because God favors a complicated relationship; instead, we had lost the ability to continue with face to face communion.

None of this was God's desire, and through Jesus, we learned to walk again with God. Jesus became approachable for all. The leper. The unbeliever. The outcast. The sinner. For me. For each of us. Jesus had come to earth as the second Adam[10] and as the perfection of the Tabernacle.[11] He pitched his symbolical tent amongst us and taught us how to live again. God had become flesh in the man Jesus.

Whereas Adam fell to sin, Jesus lived perfectly and died as the perfect sacrificial lamb. We needed one of our own to save us, and God provided his son for this very purpose.

During his life on earth, Jesus did not take on a hard-to-recognize spiritual appearance; instead, he took on flesh and blood, drew close to us, and provided victory over the flesh. He demonstrated how to live inside the human body. He taught how to think, to consider, how to process, evaluate, determine, how to act, and how to relate.

---

7. Gen 1:31, NIV
8. Refer to Exod 25:8 NIV
9. Refer to Lev 9, 10, 11 NIV
10. Refer to Rom 5:12–21, 1 Cor 15:22 NIV
11. Refer to Heb 9:21–24, Rev 21:3 NIV

A new era, our era, where Jesus overcame human desire and human temptation,[12] had commenced. By doing so, Jesus possessed the fullness of authority and authenticity to show how to live and to guide us through life. We now had someone to share our burdens and a savior to face the day. Jesus became God's self-disclosure, and our journey back to perfection had begun.

Perfect in identity, while showing compromise in character, provides the backdrop to our current state of affairs as we journey through the early years of the twenty-first century. A continuing journey of tension between that which we ought to do and that which we want to do.[13] A tension rendering us as being Flawesome.

---

12. Refer to Heb 4:15 NIV
13. Refer to Rom 7:15 NIV

2

Being Flawesome

Imagine yourself as a living house. God comes in to rebuild that house. At first, perhaps, you can understand what He is doing . . . You thought you were being made into a decent little cottage: but He is building a palace. He intends to come and live in it Himself.

C. S. Lewis[1]

Being flawesome is the fundamental philosophy of this book. Flawesome, a combination of two words. Awesome. Flawed.

God = awesome

Humanity = flawed

The simplest of gospel messages is of Jesus coming to earth to bring freedom and to live in our hearts. A story of the one called Awesome[2] choosing to love and to live within the ones who are flawed. We now continue our story as being flawesome. God in me. God in each of us.

Awesome has perhaps become too familiar in the English language, and I do hesitate in using the word awesome. After all, everything is awesome, experiences, people, food, movies, sports stars, and music. All perceived as awesome.

---

1. Lewis, *Mere Christianity*
2. Refer to Deut 7:21, NIV

These usages gravely downgrade its true meaning while offering no set framework of measurement. What is awesome to one person is unimpressive to the next person. Tomorrow's awesome movie will replace today's awesome movie. Today's awesome food maybe next year's health concern. A standard is needed to measure awesomeness. The challenge remains in that humans do not possess a standard by which to measure what is awesome, and if we could, we would disagree on the benchmark, and the standard would be ever-changing. God is awesome; the Bible informs this,[3] and God is the only measure by which awesome is determined, and God is the only one who can measure up to be awesome.

Awesome is a word to be reserved for God. This book uses the word awesome in one sense only, as attributed to God.

---

3. Refer to Deut 7:21, NIV

3

All Stories Have a Beginning

I was no longer the centre of my life and therefore I could see God in everything.

—Laura Swan[1]

All stories have a beginning. And how we get to the start is often a story in itself.

Flying over Kabul, I found myself reflecting on the broken soul of humanity. We've come a long way from Eden, and a long way from the field where Abel fell to Cain. This distance has allowed the time to develop the craft of suffering and misery and to develop new ways of shedding blood and weaponizing and often politicizing hatred for revenge and gain. We've advanced and developed, justified, and supported the continuance of the work to which Lucifer advocated, and Adam and Eve adopted.

The Hungarian proverb states it well: "Adam ate the apple, and our teeth still ache."[2]

Speaking on the new state of humanity, Jude writes: "They have followed the way of Cain who killed his brother."[3]

Adam and Eve may have been the origin of disastrous choice, but we all need to take responsibility for the continuance of this choice. It may not

1. Swan, *The Benedictine Tradition*
2. author unknown
3. Jude 11, NLV

be fruit that we are tempted by, but the fruit represented that which was forbidden. Many mysteries surround our faith, but there is clarity on areas that are prohibited. Murder. Hate. Adultery. Lust. Theft. Coveting; as with Adam and Eve, we can very easily justify our eating of that which is forbidden.

Genesis tells the story of our ancestors eating this forbidden fruit. Our ancestors had now possessed knowledge beyond their moral, ethical, spiritual, and emotional capacity to handle.

They learned to compare, and humanity's downfall set.

The flawless had become flawed.

Within one generation, the first murder took place.[4] Within several generations, humanity had become "evil,"[5] with child sacrifice[6] becoming the epitome of our descent. Adam may have initiated this calamity, but successive generations have continued, mastered, politicized, and often weaponized, and monetized this descent.

Revenge and entitlement are blights on our human race, and evidence enough of the presence of sin and evil in our world. Be it the phenomenon of road rage, the harm of revenge porn, the need for belonging demonstrated through the corruption of gang violence, communities-driven apart through neighborhood dispute, the following of tradition resulting in honor-killings. Sin has become a stain on our collective identity.

The first crewed flight by the Wright brothers was inspirational. Eight years later, the first bomb[7] dropped over the side of a plane; eight years from the culmination of knowledge, allowing humans to fly, this knowledge had become weaponized. Through flight, we sought freedom, but this freedom rested on the vulnerable foundation of humanity's collective and flawed desire to compare.

I consider that after generations of trial and error, catastrophe, and unbalanced development, we should consider our direction as a human species and take ownership of our flawed state.

Recent history provides a fascinating and telling insight to a recurring theme of every generation coming to the realization that they are living in a broken world, and they demand change as they seem to collectively grapple with essential ethical, moral, environmental, and political concerns. They are observing inconsistency with their purpose and how their and others' lives are lived. They are engaging from a root of justice and becoming

---

4. Refer to Gen 4:1–16 NIV
5. Refer to Gen 6:4–6, NIV
6. Refer to Lev 18:21, 2 Kgs 17:31, NIV

7. A hand grenade was thrown from the side of a plane piloted by Giulio Gavotti on 1 November 1911, during the Italo-Turkish War. Source: Johnston, "Libya 1911: How an Italian pilot began the air war era"

dispositioned towards a better version of what they are currently experiencing. It would seem that collectively, we are reaching this point in time again. Previous generations may have been content with this protest displayed through the arts, while other generations take to the streets. We are distressed at inequality, and we are collectively demanding change.

Unrest. Civil war. Protest. Conflict. Demonstration.

These are happening worldwide from Hong Kong to Colombia. From the streets of Paris to the streets of Baghdad. From the yellow vests to the red shirts. From religiously stoked protests in India to climate change activists in Australia. From the blood-soaked sands of Syria to the killing fields of eastern Ukraine. The cause may be different, but the intent is the same: the need for change and a collective reaction to the abuse of power. A few years back, I sat listening to a teacher lament at the challenge they were experiencing with a group of teenage boys struggling in their Christian Life studies. The curriculum was the first five books of Moses and the Kings of Israel. As my mind began to wander, I considered all of the concerns teenagers have and the growing sense of powerlessness they feel in the wake of the many huge problems that they hear about, as well as the problems they were experiencing. I considered what difference it would make if they looked at the uncompromising stand Jesus took in the wake of injustice, and how he would act in light of today's challenges. The injustice experienced by many for profitability and the plight of numerous people groups around our world. Would he speak or remain silent? The answer to this question forms the foundation of our response.

During the 1990s, the saying "What Would Jesus Do" resurfaced and gained mass popularity. It's a phrase and a challenge, a challenge not based on behavior modification, instead, a heart response to the perfected love of Jesus residing within and resulting in spiritual motivation to bring change to our external conduct. A century earlier, Sheldon had popularised this saying through the title of his best selling novel "In His Steps: What Would Jesus Do."[8] Whether it be the 1890s or the 1990s, this short phrase encapsulates the profound spiritual concept and calling of *Imitatio Christi* (imitation of Christ). Imitating Christ, through the grace of the Holy Spirit, results in perfection in love. A practice advocated by Wesley[9] as Christian perfection and a notion discussed through my writing. A perfection resulting from the perfection of Christ within, not an absolute sinless perfection.

Returning again to the story of this book.

---

8. Sheldon, *In His Steps*
9. Noble, *Holy Trinity: Holy People*

The concept originated during many long flights, most recently, a trip to Germany while absorbing Tolstoy's "The Kingdom of God Is Within You."[10] Heathrow provided the time and opportunity for a framework to be developed, refined further in Brunei, and expanded upon in Perth. But it was to be an evening in Melbourne that I achieved clarity: the relationship between comparison and doubt and the negative impact they have on the human condition.

Doubt.

Doubt is the mechanism that generates flaws in our character. Doubt that slows transformation and uncertainty that needs continuous validation and redemption. This temporal flaw in our eternal perfection.

Logically, we doubt through comparison. Should we not be able to compare, we would not need to doubt. Adam and Eve compared the forbidden fruit within the context of their perfect environment, and this led to doubt. Doubt about God's instruction, uncertainty about the hazard of the serpent's enticement, and questions about the completeness of their provision and position. They doubted their lot in life.

The serpent was subtle in approach, and we can learn insight from this subtleness. The tactics of Satan often start with doubt. It is doubting God and doubting ourselves. When uncertainty lodges in our identity, it can be manipulated and result in sin. With sin being the origin of unbelief and unbelief being the offshoot of doubt. Doubt can lay dormant within the complex framework of our minds for extended periods, muted, and waiting for trigger-points to be activated—this is the inherent danger of doubt. It is a land-mine planted for future use.

Land-mines in the physical can be described as "weapons of mass destruction in slow-motion." Weapons planted decades ago, in silence, wait for the day they are triggered to release the full potential of their destructive purpose.

---

10. Tolstoy, *The Kingdom of God*

4

Encounters with Doubt

It is a peculiar sensation, this double-consciousness, this sense of always looking at one's self through the eyes of others, of measuring one's soul by the tape of a world that looks on in amused contempt and pity.

—William Edward Burghardt Du Bois[1]

IN ALL HER IMAGERY and culture, Melbourne was alive and kicking, abuzz with the type of expectancy and energy, usually the reserve of major sporting and music events. But this is Melbourne, a vibrant city in a prosperous nation affectionately regarded as "the lucky country." Melbourne, a city of rapid growth and celebration.

The Grand Hyatt was hosting a worship event, and along with the hundreds gathered, we anticipated an evening of meeting with God; the music was electric, and the level of expectancy was high. It was in this setting that my thoughts turned towards a good friend in a new situation in the USA, and over the next 30 minutes, we communicated.

With permission granted, I'd like to share parts of our conversation to name and identify the role of doubt.

Nik   I'm praying everything goes well. Who knows what doors this will open? As God was preparing the way for Moses and Joshua, he will be with you on

---

1. Du Bois, "Strivings"

	this journey, going ahead to make the way while traveling with you as best friend, comforter, guide, and wisdom. Bless you, Tin! I'm excited for you!
Tin	Thank you for your encouraging words. I'm learning a lot but also have to deal with my old enemy of insecurity. Please pray for tomorrow.
Nik	I started to pray for you, and this came to mind; if we do nothing, we don't feel insecure. It's when we step out that these feelings emerge, yet God is there every step of the way.
Tin	Thank you so much. It's 2.23 in the morning, and I can't sleep; haunted by thoughts of "I should have said this" or "I should have said that." I'm praying but can't seem to find peace.
Nik	What-ifs and could-haves can keep us down for sure, those internal conversations that can plague us. But we take one step at a time, you said yes, you took the flight, you sat at the table God had called you to. You're at the table for a reason. I'm stoked for you if nothing else. If we're allowed hero's, you're one of mine.
Tin	Thank you so much for your comforting words, dear brother.
Nik	God brought a young Vietnamese boy fleeing with his family, from the deck of a refugee ship to sit at the table with some of the world's greatest influencers. Quite the story. Quite the God.
Tin	Thank you so much, my dear friend.
Nik	I've been considering our message conversation from Sunday. I wanted to write more, but it was during worship. Where you shared about your old enemy of "insecurity," I wanted to share my enemy of "insignificance." Between the two of us, we probably make a whole. I can feel secure but insignificant, and you can feel insecure, but you have great significance. Perhaps we should put our skills and talents together and start a movement of "living imperfectly perfect."
Tin	Wow, that sounds like a pretty fantastic plan.

This conversation led to the writing of this book. Although the concept of this book had been developing over recent years, resulting in my earlier book[2] on identity, this Melbourne night reinforced my thoughts and became the transition to consolidated confidence. I couldn't shake the question of being made in the image of a perfect God how can we still struggle with insignificance and insecurity?

Doubt.

Doubt in our identity. We both were experiencing significant doubts of insecurity and insignificance.

To doubt, unfortunately, is to be human.

2. Matthews, *The Nine Veils*

Doubt is a condition we experience while living in a flawed environment. It remains a temporal reality that will evaporate at our resurrection but remains a treacherous landscape to navigate through.

Although doubting does not impact our identity nor impact our salvation, we none the less project doubt through our character, and this projection of character tends to rise above our identity. People tend to review us through character rather than identity, and the world tends to compare us on qualifications and skills. The devil will cultivate the negative aspects of our character to raise doubt and comparison in others' lives.

Doubt resonates from disorientation. We see this exemplified in the Psalms, a collection of writings that explore faith and doubt.

The Psalms shed light on human exposure to doubt with several Psalms exposing the dark realms of the mind. We discover the author finding the freedom to lament their pain, name their anguish, and identify their confusion while revealing their disorientation to God's mystery and finding the freedom to cry out for help. God inclines his ear to the Psalmist. I develop a picture of God moving closer as the lament gets darker, God leaning in with his ear towards the Psalmist to hear the cry of the heart while ready at an instance to wrap his arms around the Psalmist and bring great comfort through a floodgate of response. God is not shy towards our lament, or our doubt.

Doubt without hope will lead to deeper depths of despair, whereas hope allows us to gaze beyond the horizon full of expectancy.

At its root, doubt is a manifestation of unbelief, and we doubt because we lack an understanding of God in his fullness, and we underestimate the perfect life offered. For the follower of Jesus, discernment replaces doubt. We do not enter situations and utilize doubt as a decision-making tool; instead, we engage discernment to gain insight as to what is going on.

Doubt will influence our abilities and cast shadows on our identity. Doubt also has the potential to cause negative behavioral responses, and advocates for the often-agonizing questions centered on one's self. Doubt will also rob the experience of God's promise of full provision.

Doubt for the follower of Jesus may result in a lack of conviction to fully participate in the Great Commission and to advance the kingdom of Heaven, stemming from our lack of understanding of the basics of our belief; or, because we underestimate the reach of Jesus to meet our particular needs. Perhaps doubt creeps in through our tolerance to a society postured with a growing intolerance to the message of Jesus.

We doubt our faith. We doubt our belief. We doubt our assurance.

We conclude that our life is the sum-total of our behavior rather than the wholeness of our identity. In this scenario, we can experience salvation, but we do not experience the fullness of liberation, and doubt weakens our faith.

We all doubt, and it is our response to doubt that can benefit or jeopardize. It is this wrongful response to personal doubt that is indicative of being flawed in our character.

We also need to separate a healthy response to dissatisfaction and doubt.

Wilberforce, much dissatisfied with slavery. Martin Luther King Jr, exceedingly distressed with discrimination. Nightingale's discontent with poor medical conditions. The list goes on.

Their dissatisfaction became an essential motivator for change, whereas doubt promotes unbelief.

5

Being Perfect

This is the very perfection of a man, to find out his own imperfections.

—Augustine[1]

A DIVINE MYSTERY OF our flawed existence is the concept of our perfection.

Perfection is not so much an ideal we are aiming for, or a destination we are traveling towards, or a system of judgment whereby we can quickly determine each other's progress against a fabricated Perfection-Continuum. Nor is it an achievement to pursue, or license granted to be a perfectionist. Perfection is an attitude and a knowledge of being perfected through the completed work of Jesus in our lives. Perfection is the confidence in knowing our identities are based on God's perfection and not on human behavior. It's the position of our hearts and the motivation of our minds aligned to the character of God.

The beauty of our perfection is we can't grow any more perfect. We can only discover the fullness of perfection realized in our lives, and as we find out these benefits, our lives become complete, and we achieve a higher purpose. Perfection is our identity, and we do not need to sell ourselves cheaply by giving people a discounted version of our perfection. We exhibit this discount every time we devalue ourselves.

---

1. Augustine, as quoted on Goodreads

Perhaps the greatest gift we can offer humanity is our authenticity, authentic living where we understand the fullness of our identity, the fullness of our purpose, and the ability to live life in the fullness of the spirit.

Referring to the human in the same context of perfection would lead many to summarise a contradiction of terms, especially when we personalize "human" with ourselves. Yet, we are called perfect, and throughout scripture, God calls us to be perfect.[2]

Perfect is who we are. It is our identity, perfected in Jesus.

God is the measure of perfection and attempts to produce perfection will fail. Sin has reduced humanity to imperfection, and the pursuit of manufactured human perfection will forever fall-short; yet, many do drive to attain this unreachable concept and the abstract notion of finding inner perfection. We often applaud this pursuit.

We can only gain perfection by allowing Jesus to be perfect on our behalf by voluntarily entering the transformational process of being made perfect.[3] We trade our sin and our guilt for the perfect love of Jesus, and by doing so, we are sanctified and justified and gain right standing with God.

Our efforts cannot produce perfection, nor can our behavior maintain perfection. Perfection is a gift extended in our flawed state, and we now have the responsibility to live our lives in exact alignment with our reality, learning to live from perfected identity rather than from our imperfection. And this is why discipleship is of utmost importance to the follower of Jesus. Inner change is at the heart of discipleship, and outward acts of kindness are our response to this inward change.

Our actions do not save us, but our efforts will inevitably influence others: friends, colleagues, and the stranger who watches our behavior. Deep down, we are probably all people-watchers. We observe and watch people. We do this on the bus, on the plane, in the coffee shop; we can't help ourselves. We see, compare, and contrast. As followers of Jesus, we are on display, and our responsibility is to allow people to see the beauty of the love of Jesus shining in us and through us. When we fail in this responsibility, we do provide a compromised version of Jesus, and our lives do become a contradiction in terms.

Tolstoy reflects on this apparent contradiction exhibited within humans. An inconsistency whereby humans act in a contrary way to how their conscience is leading. Tolstoy concludes on this contradiction as "the great struggle we all face."

---

2. Refer to Matt 5:48; 1 Pet 1:15–16; Heb 10:14, NIV
3. Refer to Rom 12:2, 2 Cor 3:18, Col 3:9–10, NIV

Our whole life is in flat contradiction with all we know, and with all we regard as necessary and right. This contradiction runs through everything, in economic life, in political life, and in international life. As though we had forgotten what we knew and put away for a time the principles we believe in (we cannot help still believing in them because they are the only foundation we have to base our life on) we do the very opposite of all that our conscience and our common sense require of us.[4]

Tolstoy finds alignment to what Paul explains firstly in Romans:

I do not understand what I do. For what I want to do I do not do, but what I hate I do.[5]

And expounded further in Galatians where Paul describes this pull of the flesh versus the pull of the spirit:

For the flesh desires what is contrary to the Spirit, and the Spirit what is contrary to the flesh. They are in conflict with each other, so that you are not to do whatever you want.[6]

While navigating this contradiction, we need to be aware of the exhibition of our flawed character being on display to a watching world, where the results of poor external behavior exhibited, in response to God's perfection, produces the contradiction in our lives that Tolstoy and the Apostle Paul discuss.

We generally do exhibit our character over our identity, and it is our character that typically defines who we are to this watching world. Viewed by the world as flawed yet recognized by Heaven as being perfect, and this is where contradiction is externalized through our habits undermining our identity. We do not lose our salvation, but our character, driven by contradiction, can appear as anything other than redeemed, and navigating this reality is discipleship.

Therefore, the follower of Jesus needs humility and speedy response to their wrong behavior. To ask for forgiveness and to not hide fault, or to not continue the practice of shift-blaming that started in Eden. Our identity needs to take a far more prominent role than that of our behavior.

Having perfection reside in our life secures our identity. Having perfection demonstrated through our character is the journey of discipleship.

---

4. Tolstoy, *The Kingdom of God*
5. Rom 7:16, NIV
6. Gal 5:17, NIV

We all stumble every day,[7] countless times, and it is our character that succumbs to the reality of imperfection.

Feelings and emotions become hijacked by our character, and thoughts toward our physical attributes, rather than generated from our identity. We make a mistake, and we feel a failure. We have a negative response to the image reflected through the mirror, and we feel inferior. We fight to the top, and we feel superior. We get praised for academic abilities, and pride makes an entry. We soon become the sum-total of our thoughts and feelings toward ourselves, a self-imposed grading system that jeopardizes our reality. Below the skin and behind the thought is the real you.

Loved. Cherished. Valued. Known. Needed.

Of the greatest of human need is the need to be seen and the need to be known. This need can only be met in fulness by the God of love who is all-seeing and all-knowing. God, who would say, "I know you." "I see you." "I feel you." "I love you." It is within this reality that the human finds purpose and meaning to life.

The need for fulfillment in each of these desires is intrinsic to the human condition. We need to be loved. We need to be cherished. We need to be valued. We need to be known. We need to be needed. We need to be seen. God provides not only the fullness of life but also the answers to life. Inherently, we are curious creatures, and we need to discover our origin and our identity as well as our destination. Jesus came to bring life in its fullness, and heaven guarantees perfection for eternity.

In God, we have been set up for success rather than for failure. God knows us intimately, and the Bible talks of God knowing us before we were born.[8]

We do not shock God. We cannot shock God.

God knows us, and God considered us worthy of redemption. Contemporary language can oft place an over-emphasis on the unworthiness of humans as to receiving anything from God. While being true, such over-emphasis of our unworthiness can become unhealthy and lead to seeds of low self-worth and low self-esteem sewn, generating a narrative of being of little value. Being unworthy of God's love perhaps has more to do with there being nothing we can offer in return for God's love, and all we can do is receive. The essence of God's love is how his love is free, flying in the face of systems whereby people are valued on their economic potential either as a purchaser or contributor, and many situations we find ourselves in are talent-based. We would rarely receive a job offer if not for our education,

---

7. Refer to Jas 3:2 NIV
8. Refer to Ps 139:13–16, Jer 1:5, NIV

qualification, or our ability to be productive. We are not worthy in that we have nothing of worth to be traded for God's free and precious gift of love, and all we can do is receive. This does not devalue humans; instead, it takes the emphasis away from our efforts and places the work of redemption rightly with God.

The NLV puts this concept beautifully:

> But—
> When God our Savior revealed his kindness and love, he saved us, not because of the righteous things we had done, but because of his mercy. He washed away our sins, giving us a new birth and new life through the Holy Spirit. He generously poured out the Spirit upon us through Jesus Christ our Savior. Because of his grace he made us right in his sight and gave us confidence that we will inherit eternal life.[9]

We can devalue our lives by evoking a sense of false-humility as it relates to our unworthiness. God does not make mistakes, and he did not make his first mistake with any of us. This should instill the most significant measure of confidence. We desperately need this confidence generated from our perfection.

Were it not possible to gain the confidence of this perfection it would not have been said. Nor was it meant to:

- Tease us
- Suppress us
- Create a hierarchy of perceived perfection
- Set an unreachable standard to be unjustly judged against
- Remind us, through each thought, that we are not good enough

We see a theme running through the life of Jesus, whereby he challenged religious leaders who became engaged in creating hierarchies of perfection and casting judgment on those who did not measure up to these designed systems of comparison.[10] A measure that they broke time and time again. They were the human face of hypocrisy. By determining and valuing individual lives, they were going against all that Jesus came to fulfill. The opposite of this is to be found on the journey of discipleship.

---

9. Titus 3:4–7, NLV
10. Refer to Matt 23 NIV

6

Pursuing Perfection and the Journey of Discipleship

Man: a being in search of meaning.

—Plato[1]

Human growth and development are of high importance to God, as is the case with every parent. A parent's desire is for the healthy growth and development of their child, and this priority would often see a sacrifice made for their child. There is a strange phenomenon that happens at the birth of a child; something so small and fragile becomes the most loved.

The author of the book of Hebrews provides a simple, but profound, word picture detailing natural growth while adding a spiritual principle:

> By now you should be teachers. Instead, you need someone to teach you again the first things you need to know from God's Word. You still need milk instead of solid food. Anyone who lives on milk cannot understand the teaching about being right with God. He is a baby. Solid food is for full-grown men. They have learned to use their minds to tell the difference between good and bad.[2]

---

1. Hourly History, *Greek Mythology*
2. Heb 5:12–14, NLV

The second part of verse 14 assumes how "they have learned to use their minds"; in this occurrence, it was to differentiate the good from the bad. Other translations use the terms "trained themselves," or, "their senses exercised," and "discernment trained" to argue the need for voluntary involvement in human development.

It is natural, and it's spiritual to seek growth; our bodies and our minds point towards this developmental need. Some growth is involuntary (height and features as examples), while some of this growth gained through voluntary exposure (such as learning and relationships). Our minds are an integral part of who we are, and lovingly, God cares for the state of our minds. We can, therefore, conclude that we worship God, and we relate to God with every aspect of our lives; our mind, our strength, our very being. And for this reason, it becomes essential that we find wholeness within our mind, our body, and our soul.

After all, following Jesus is not a passive activity, nor is it a spectator's pursuit. It requires effort and choice. It involves every part of who we are to be in alignment with God's good and perfect plan for our lives.[3] It requires that we do not entertain false gods and that we do not chase after temptation. It requires bringing our lives into submission to the Lordship of Christ; while realizing that this submission is actually for our benefit. Areas of our lives that remain outside of God's plans will cause us to struggle and to fail through life.

Life is a constant state of transition, and the Bible speaks about these movements, starting with the transition from Eden to the outside world. The transition from a patriarchal society to a society governed through the Judges, and transitioning through to the Kings. Israel's transition from nomadic wanderers to slavery, to a nation in their own right, through to captivity and liberation. The transition from the prophets of old to the greatest of prophets; John the Baptist. The transition from the law to grace. The transition from Jesus walking with us to the sending of the Holy Spirit to live within us.

At a personal level, our bodies transition from youth to old age; our muscles grow and then decline. For the fortunate ones, kindergarten transitions to school, transitions to college, transitions to university, transitions to work, transitions to a promotion, transitions to retirement. Then on a grand scale, our human species is transitioning from the temporal to the eternal.

After turning to Jesus, the most significant transition is from following Jesus to becoming a disciple of Jesus.

---

3. Refer to Jer 29:11, Prov 3:5–6, Rom 8:28, Eph 5:15–16, 1 Tim 6:6, Matt 6:33, Phil 1:6, NIV

The journey of discipleship is a journey we need to take if we are to be capable and whole, and it is a journey of relationship and discovery rather than a goal-driven pursuit or a journey to arrive at a final destination only.

The Apostle Paul likens this journey to that of a race, and at the commencement of this race, we become champions and receive the winner's prize. It is a race in reverse, however, where the winners' ceremony happens before the race starts, and we step up to the victors' podium to receive the crown[4] in advance of effort employed and the sound of the start-gun. We then enter this race as one who has gained victory with the winner's crown in place. And because we have all won, and there is no need for competition, we can run and help others along the way. Yet, the journey still needs to be run, requiring discipline, persistence, and endurance.

Regardless of how hard we try, we are unable to reach this preferred future by ourselves; indeed, maintaining a self-centric lifestyle will create hurdles and will place obstacles along the journey. We may hobble over the finish line, with the winners crown still in place, but with the heartache and pain of running the race with the regret of achieving poor behavior and creating the torment of broken relationships along the way.

The journey of discipleship, being the race we run, will lead to the discovery of identity, and a growing understanding of the fullness of the knowledge of Jesus experienced through relationship. As we grow closer towards the love of God, we learn of his love for us; and in doing so, we learn of God's love for others.

While our liberated identity is perfected, our character can remain, at times, shocking. Discipleship, therefore, is aligning our character to our faith, giving up our rights, and inviting Jesus as Lord of our lives beyond the point of salvation.

We need to recognize Jesus as Lord, and we need to make Jesus Lord.

---

4. Refer to 1 Cor 9:24–27, NIV

7

Recognizing and Making Jesus Lord

If everyone is thinking alike, then somebody isn't thinking.
—General George S. Patton[1]

In First Timothy, the Apostle Paul sets out a challenge. A challenge that is passable and a challenge that we must engage should we desire to live life to the fullest and to make Jesus Lord of our lives. It promotes a lifestyle of Lordship—a lifestyle of multiple choices, of discipleship, and of moving forward.

> But you, man of God, flee from all this, and pursue righteousness, godliness, faith, love, endurance and gentleness. Fight the good fight of the faith.[2]

Held within this short passage is a wealth of insight
But you. A personal charge and instruction, written to each of us.
man of God. The deepest of identity statements that we are "of God." We are made in the image of God;[3] woman and man.
flee. Requiring affirmative action, running away from all that would harm us.

---

1. Patton, as qouted on Goodreads
2. 1 Tim 6:11–12, NIV
3. Refer to Gen 1:27, NIV

from all this. A personal fill-in-the-blank statement. We do have generalised areas we need to run from; violence, anger, and greed, to name a few; while having particular areas, we need to flee. And several of these areas will be harmful to some and not harmful to others, such as addictive tendencies towards technology, gaming, and alcohol. On occasions, this will be to flee from real places. If a particular environment stirs trouble, then we become wise to avoid these areas.[4]

and pursue. Similar to flee, this is an affirmative command. Pursue what is good. Run towards that which is right. Paul gives examples of such; *righteousness, godliness, faith, love, endurance, and gentleness.*

Within this passage, we discern the link between humans possessing freedom of choice yet without the ability to determine the consequence of this freedom. At Eden, we learned how to internalize our freewill, and we identified freewill as being beneficial to serve our own individualized needs; whereas, freewill operates for the exact opposite reason; the external purpose of being able to love outwardly. This learned individualization and internalization of freewill became a blight for all future generations. We call this selfishness and self-centric living.

We can flee, or we can remain, but the consequence is out of our control.

The foundation of discipleship is the ability to make good choices. Although these decisions do become more natural as we build healthy habits and lifestyles, it does remain impossible to live by the standards of discipleship without the Holy Spirit active in our lives.

The message of the Bible is "Jesus Christ is Lord," and the Lordship of Christ is framed within his relationship to us. Lordship generally depicts a position of authority and speaks of dominion and rulership. Of one holding supreme power, and this is true regarding God. Yet, this same God humbled himself before humans and voluntarily gave his life for us in the most tragic of circumstances. God has all dominion and all authority and mandates this rule through a loving relationship with us. In an almost twist to this divine status of God, he chooses to share the responsibility with us, to welcome us as co-heirs.[5] To empower us and to liberate us.[6] We become family members of God.

Within this context, God remains sovereign without the need to be controlling.

---

4. Principles found in Prov 1:1–19, Prov 5, 7, Rom 16:17, 1 Cor 6:18, 1 Cor 10:14, NIV

5. Refer to Rom 8:17, NIV

6. Refer to Gal 5:1, Gal 5:13, 1 Pet 2:16, NIV

Our responsibility is to recognize Jesus as Lord and to acknowledge Jesus as Lord. It is also our responsibility to recognize sin and temptation in our lives and recognize the availability and proximity of sin and temptation to our lives. We do this through the power of the Holy Spirit.

Making Jesus Lord is the giving up of everything that acts as barriers to realizing the fulness of God in our lives. It's getting rid of that which would hold us back while inviting the fullness of the Holy Spirit to dwell in our lives. It requires that we live from a place of victory, a minute-by-minute lifestyle made up of thousands of individual choices. As we gain victory in the foothills of our lives, success then focuses on the higher ground, until total victory through Jesus is achieved.

To reject addictive behavior and harmful narratives is a battle. Descriptions such as we are unlovable, and we are of no worth. These strongholds of self-perception can be amongst the hardest to conquer as it requires a level of vulnerability that we are not all that comfortable with. It requires an awareness of being deeply loved by God solely for who we are and not for what we are, or for what we have, simply who we are.

The Lordship of Christ is the understanding that Jesus has completed his work, and the level of freedom we experience will be dependent on the depth of healing we are willing to accept. We progress through allowing the Holy Spirit to pinpoint the high ground in our lives, those areas not in surrender to Jesus. Making Jesus Lord is, after the point of salvation, the greatest of priorities.

In not making Jesus Lord does not impact his love for us. Jesus's love has already been given and assured. Instead, it is the depth of experiencing the fullness of his love and the renewing power of his desire to transform our lives radically that we miss. By not making Jesus Lord, and through the placing of things to a higher level of priority in our lives, is the planting of a seed that will lead to future disappointment and temptation. These seeds are empowered when, at a point of disorientation to God's love, we look for alternatives to satisfy that which only God can fulfill.

Although this does not affect God's love for us, it will impact the effectiveness of our calling. I do become convinced, the more I observe, the numbers of followers of Jesus failing to grasp the full meaning of their lives. I see this introspectively as I look at wasted years of my own experience, and extrovertedly in the lives of others. It remains entirely possible for the follower of Jesus to be loved by God while continuing to live a dull and mediocre life, a life not making any real impact on the furtherance of humanity. Should we fail to discover the fullness of our identity, we will remain unclear about the fullness of our purpose.

It's a case of giving up and picking up. It's a positive experience. We let go of our baggage, and we become increasingly empowered by the Holy Spirit. God's love is unconditional, and this unconditional love provides the framework of living. How our lives are built upon this absolute foundation is very much conditional on the choices and actions each of us takes. Out of his pure love for us, God would generally not build a spiritual vocation on a weak foundation. This being out of love and not out of punishment.

Jesus does not need to do anything new, as he has accomplished everything already. What does need to happen, however, is for each of us to align our lives, totally, with Jesus. To identify the high ground in our lives, and to make Jesus Lord in all areas of our life.

I, therefore, pose a question. How? How to make Jesus Lord of my life, and how do I recognize high ground in my life that remain strongholds against Jesus?

Recognize is an observational word implying there's a possibility of not recognizing. We are created to think, process, determine, and compare. To be able to recognize Jesus requires both observation and discernment. By default, to be able to recognize something would require alternatives to be regarded, and it is often the volume and disguise of these alternatives that hide the need for Jesus. It is most likely that we are not actively rebelling against the Lordship of Christ; simply, we have learned to become numb to the need. Alternatively, our attention turns elsewhere, and we choose the good over the perfect.

Make is a choice. We decide to make a coffee. We choose to start a training course, and we decide to make Jesus Lord. The alternative is not to make Jesus Lord.

We choose.

We need to be aware, however, that for each choice we make there is a consequence. The greater the choice, the higher the consequence. We may choose to ignore our alarm clock and face the result of being late to work or having to miss breakfast. We may decide to ignore Jesus and face the consequence of life without Jesus. Although the result of our choice remains outside our control, we have the knowledge that Jesus has removed the guilt from our wrong decisions by becoming our scape-goat.[7] Human hands were laid on him so that he can carry the consequence of human sin. This is how a condemned prisoner can have liberation for eternity while remaining locked up in the temporary.

And for us to face temptation, there needs to be a tempter. Although temptation can have a firm grip on a person's life, especially when ingrained

---

7. Refer to Heb 9:11–10:17 NIV

through years of exposure, the good news of Jesus is how the power of temptation is defeated.[8]

Light is most visible when contrasted against the darkness, and it is often through the times of crisis, or the times in which we do not know in which way to turn, that Jesus enters and light floods in, and at this juncture, we have the choice. To walk through the door or stay in the dark. Walking through the door requires leaving baggage behind, and this is the struggle when we have grown dependent and familiar with what the baggage represents to us. The Bible references the role of idols throughout, and the idols of biblical times will most likely appear different from our idols.

An idol is a thing or person holding a level of control over our lives whereby to turn from them would cause a sense of loss, or where they possess the ability to influence our emotions and our sense of wellbeing negatively. Examples would include the obvious; money, screen-time, drugs, and excessive use of alcohol. Less obviously, relationships where unhealthy dependency and boundaries are not established and are now degrading our quality of life.

An idol occupies the ground where a deficiency is felt.

When we experience emptiness in our lives, when we give credence to feelings of doubt, we can all too easily start acting from a position of deficiency. In God, there is no deficiency, and one day we will experience God in fullness. Still, until that day comes, we will remain tempted to alleviate these feelings of lack with consumables, wealth, experience, and people. In doing so, we place these above God, often unwittingly, and we may not realize the full extent of that with which we are doing.

Unfortunately, we all do experience deficiency to one degree or another, and therefore we experience the traveling companion of deficiency; temptation. Ignorance is no excuse, and God's grace is all-sufficient, even in the face of our ignorance.

The role of unwarranted deficiency is perhaps best observed in the story of the Prodigal Son.[9] The younger son experienced weakness early on in the story and recklessly chased an elusive answer to his poorly perceived condition. As the story develops, we meet the older brother who stayed home and who could have voluntarily enjoyed daily and continuous communion with his father. This older brother lacked not a thing.[10]

Two brothers. Two stories of deficiency. Two responses.

---

8. Refer to Heb 4:15, NIV
9. Refer to Luke 15:11–32 NIV
10. Refer to Luke 15:25–31, NIV

The younger brother acted out his impulse by placing a barrier between himself and his father, and by doing so, faced humility. Attitude, geography, and choice led to his downfall, and humility, hope, and decision led to his reunion. He was perhaps a rebel who externalized his deficiency. The older brother, it can be assumed, shared a commonality of attitude and choice, but maintained proximity. His opinion of life not being fair[11] most likely led to a deficiency in his understanding of all that he had. He lacked not a thing but still allowed temptation to generate a feeling of scarcity while his stupor and wallowing degraded his perspective further, rendering his heart aggrieved.

The older brother seemed to have internalized his passivity, and at some juncture in the story, dwelling in this deficiency and experiencing rejection, he lost communion while proximity was maintained. He exhibited a common flaw in his identity, whereby he postured his heart to adopt a narrative of "it's not fair, what about my needs." His identity became hijacked through comparison, resulting in him being unable to comprehend the fullness of his inheritance.

Jesus promises each of us: "all power and authority I give to you."[12] Should we fail to live in the fullness of our identity, we, like the older brother, will miss out on the completeness of our inheritance.

One a story of rebellion. The other a tale of rejection. Both an account of deficiency.

When we gain momentum from growing confidence and strengthening in our resolve, that within the kingdom of God, there is no lack nor deficiency, our identity is assured. The lure of temptation weakens in comparison to the fullness that is ours. Temptation has no hold and can no longer rival what we already have. It is when we stray away from God that temptation works. It is when we reject fullness and embrace deficiency that temptation does its job, and we allow compromise to take root in our lives.

An unhealthy relationship to comparison leaves much space for vulnerability to erode our sense of worth and value while providing loaded triggers not just to undermine our lives, but the lives of others as we succumb to jealousy and greed, being the dangerous travel companions of comparison.

---

11. Refer to Luke 15:28–30, NIV
12. Matt 28:18, Luke 10:19, NIV

8

Comparison

Strong desires held us in their power. We wanted only to please ourselves. We wanted what others had and were angry when we could not have them. We hated others and they hated us.

—The Bible (NLV)[1]

Self-determining the requirements and attributes of our identity will require an absolute or at least a benchmark to compare. This need for comparison becomes a journey towards an elusive horizon, where the background becomes ambiguous as society evolves to new requirements for acceptance. The problem of God is that he is the definition of *absolute* in a context where relativity and experience are highly valued. When we engage in comparison, a standard is required, and how this standard is determined becomes all-important. When these standards shift, we are left with the need to recalibrate. We recalibrate, and the standard has changed once more, needing further recalibration. This becomes repetitive and is no way to live.

Comparison can then turn negative as we become dependent on the need to compare as the means to determine our progress in this world. A negative contrast can lead some, even nations, postured towards rebellion. While leading others postured towards rejection, and still, others postured towards resignation. This posturing will reside and manifest within the

1. Titus 3:3, NLV

mind, and this can result in physical displays of the outworking of the mind. Bullying and intimidation. Self-harm and the lowering of self-esteem. Nation raging against nation.

A sure way to offer the world a discounted version of our perfection is through comparison and the engaging of Imposter Syndrome that will further undermine the discovery of our perfected identity.

Comparison.

Some comparison is beneficial (consider the child needing to understand the difference between hot and cold water; the need to compare our life without Jesus with the hope of being with Jesus) but comparison has a real capacity to work against us. The human journey with comparison dates back to Eden, where we were presented with a choice; to compare fruit and to develop our response.

The New Testament emphasizes comparison in the form of how-to and how-not-to live commands.[2] Yet, comparison, when coupled with a poor self-image, has the devastating power to create negative consequences where this comparison is attributed to the problems of this world. The negative impact of comparison will undoubtedly manifest in complaining and coveting, which through time can quickly turn to rage and hatred, externally directed towards society at large, toward specific groupings, or aimed at individuals. Alternatively, comparison can be internalized, building a narrative where we take on the role of a victim, and we carry the toxic emotions that accompany victimhood.

Being well aware of the link between comparison and sin, Jesus, through his first recorded public address[3] taught us how to live lives free from deficiency, and comparison:

- Do not anger
- Do not lust
- Do not compare what you have with what you do not have

Unfortunately, history provides, for example after example of toxic comparison.

---

2. Examples include: Matt 5:3–7:7, Matt 18:10, Matt 23:1–33, John 3:16, Rom 2:1–4, Rom 12:9–21, Rom 13:1, Rom 13:8–14, Rom 14:1, Rom 14:10–12, 1 Cor 3:16–17, 1 Cor 6:19–20, 1 Cor 9:24–27, 1 Cor 15:34, 2 Cor 10:5, Gal 5:16–26, Gal 6:1–3, Gal 6:7–8, Eph 4:1–6, Eph 4:11–15, Eph 4:25–26, Eph 4:31–32, Eph 5:1–8, Phil 2:2–8, Col 3:5–10, 1 Thess 3:12–13, 2 Thess 2:1–3, 1 Tim 4:8, Heb 13:1–3, Heb 13:5, Heb 13:15–16, Heb 13:18, Jas 1:5, Jas 1:19–20, Jas 1:22–27, Jas 2:1, Jas 2:14–24, Jas 4:1, Jas 4:11–12, 1 Pet 2:21, 1 John 1:9 NIV

3. Refer to Matt 5, 6, 7, NIV

COMPARISON

The Fall of Lucifer

Lucifer compared his position in God's kingdom and was not satisfied. He invented an imaginary place of significance for himself, and he desired to be like God.[4] We have limited knowledge of the identity of angels and how they function. Still, we do know Lucifer was an exceedingly beautiful angel.[5] He was an anointed cherub[6] and possibly the highest of all other angels,[7] yet, through comparison, he lusted for more.

The prophets Isaiah[8] and Ezekiel[9] provide a rare glimpse at, and a symbolic insight into, Lucifer's problem of comparison, and into the dynamics of the angelic nation. Isaiah and Ezekiel refer specifically to the Kings of Babylon and Tyre, but in doing so, they do reference the power behind both kings, Lucifer, and his motivation. He viewed God through a framework of comparison, and this comparison led to his fall.

The Fall of Humanity

Adam and Eve compared the forbidden fruit with all other fruit. We know the story well. They compared, and they chose wrongly. Interestingly, the comparison of Adam and Eve has many similarities to the comparison Lucifer had with God. Lucifer wanted to be like God,[10] and Adam and Eve wanted the same knowledge as God.[11] In both examples, Lucifer, and Adam and Eve, were not confident in their identity. They wrongly believed they needed more, needed more than their perfection to allow themselves to live their desired lives, the lives they felt entitled to.

The serpent was cunning and was able to entice Adam and Eve to look inwards towards a fabricated deficiency, to then look outward towards a source of fulfillment that would meet their perceived lack, a deficiency based on two wrong assumptions

They needed more.

They deserved more.

Satan, through documented and observable predatory behavior, will zone into our perceived need and vulnerability. He will focus on our psychological and emotional needs, and he will explore ways to influence us and to advocate that we push our triggers of deficiency. We will push the

---

4. Refer to Isa 14:12–14, NIV
5. Refer to Ezek 28:17, NIV
6. Refer to Ezek 28:14, NIV
7. Refer to Ezek 28:14; Isa 14:12, NIV
8. Refer to Isa 14, NIV
9. Refer to Ezek 28, NIV
10. Refer to Isa 14:13–14, NIV
11. Refer to Gen 3:4–7, NIV

triggers through the result of varying reasons; unhealthy inquiry, voyeurism, lack of self-worth, lack of value, and a poor understanding of our identity, to name a few.

Through accomplishing this action, he will have achieved his desired delivery of detrimental and disturbing realities into our spiritual walk.

From the Fall of Adam and Eve to the challenge of the twenty-first century, the modus operandi of Satan has common themes. Namely, normalizing that which is wrong, advocating for the pursuit of what is forbidden, agitating the human soul to desire what is not needed, and confusing freedom with bondage. Sin becomes entertainment and recreational, and normalized in many cultures where we have lost our collective moral anchor. It is the same story, just appearing different on the surface. Satan does have a signature pattern that he follows.

Following their terrible choice, Adam and Eve experienced perceived deficiency in their bodies.[12] The Bible tells how they looked to cover themselves. We can surmise on this being in response to their hiding from God; this is true. Yet, there is much room to consider that they compared each other, imagined deficiency, and covered themselves. They lost confidence in their physical appearance, and they experienced what is quite possibly the first recorded instance of relational awkwardness between the two genders.[13]

Adam and Eve's fall unleashed much into our existence, and we have adopted much of this to our collective story, comparison, tension, and the defense-mechanism of blame-shifting. Adam blamed Eve,[14] Eve blamed the serpent,[15] and the serpent misrepresented God.[16] We continue this trend by looking for ways to excuse poor behavior; we blame our upbringing, we blame our teachers, our governments, our addictions, our circumstances, or we blame the advice of others. Instead of taking ownership of our own poor decisions, we deploy this defense mechanism of blame-shifting. This is why repentance is hard. Repentance requires the shift of blame away from others and on ourselves.

We can blame the devil and the evil he uses for the troubles our world faces, yet, any in-depth investigation would soon discover human fingerprints all over these troubles.

Life could have been different if Adam and Eve humbly admitted their guilt and received the forgiveness available through the one who remained

---

12. Refer to Gen 3:17, 10 NLT
13. Refer to Gen 3:12, NIV
14. Refer to Gen 3:12, NIV
15. Refer to Gen 3:13 NIV
16. Refer to Gen 3:1–5, NIV

in the Garden,[17] and the one who, even in the absence of their humility, provided for their immediate need of covering their shame.[18]

Adam and Eve were the ideal representation of humanity. They were born from God, born from perfection with perfect identity and perfect DNA. Born with flawless skin, perfect bones, excellent features, born into an ideal climate and environment, with perfect food. In Genesis 2, we read:

> Adam and his wife were both naked, and they felt no shame.[19]

By Genesis 3, we learn:

> At that moment their eyes were opened, and they suddenly felt shame at their nakedness.[20]

In just one short period, humanity had become hijacked by comparison, and compromised by doubt, allowing shame, poor self-esteem, and low self-worth, into our existence. God's validation remains that we are "very good," and our response to God's validation sheds light on our appreciation of God, and our acceptance of ourselves. The link between these two validations (God and self) are fundamental to successful living.

When we are not at peace with God, we are not at peace with ourselves.

When we cannot love God, we struggle to love ourselves.

When we consider there is no hope in God, then we will continuously search for hope.

When we consider God is not living, then we will struggle to comprehend the purpose and meaning of life.

Because God is peace, God is love, God is hope, and God is life, we will struggle through life when attempts are made to live without God. Akin to trying to breathe but failing to find oxygen within the air.

People often hate the idea of God, and in our western societies, this hatred towards the idea of God grows. Yet, when we discover the person of God and exchange our hatred for amazement, our very lives are transformed as we open the door to peace, love, hope, and life. By abandoning collective hostility towards the idea of God and being collectively amazed at the person of God, this will transform our world.

In the absence of this, we self-validate through the filter of our deficiency, and this will often result in relegating ourselves to a lowly position, jeopardizing our well-being, and becoming detrimental to our identity.

---

17. Refer to Gen 3:8, NIV
18. Refer to Gen 3:21 NIV
19. Gen 2:25, NIV
20. Gen 3:7, NLT

Alternatively, this self-validation will elevate the strong and weaken the poor. This is the consequence God was revealing when he counseled Israel from choosing a strong man to be their King.[21]

The result of the Fall of Adam and Eve led to the serpent's curse,[22] and the consequences of the fall described to Adam and Eve.[23] God did not curse Adam and Eve in Eden; instead, God was explaining the process of action and consequence. Through the exile from Eden, God provided for the continuance of humanity while immediately setting in motion the protoevangelium of Genesis 3:15. Humans have been and will continue to be the most loved and the most cherished[24] of God's creation. This is the basis of our identity. Love.

Unfortunately, this same sense of deficiency continues to impact humans today. As is the case with Adam and Eve, we somehow conclude that we are deficient, and we need to find completeness. Completeness in our lives and integrity in our identity, to find meaningful community, to prove our worth, and to experience true connectedness.

There is deep deceit that can occupy the minds of those who seek greatness, and this deceit is found in the boundary of truth and lies, where we start to believe our cause and find a reason to justify our actions. When things then do go wrong, we can become quick to apportion blame and to shift blame.

A case in point is that of the biblical account of Adonijah.[25] Adonijah, the son of Haggith[26] and the fourth son of King David,[27] rose to compete for the throne of Israel in a direct challenge to King David and his son, Solomon. Adonijah positioned himself and postured himself for greatness.

> Then Adonijah the son of Haggith exalted himself, saying, "I will be king"; and he prepared for himself chariots and horsemen, and fifty men to run before him.[28]

Adonijah, out of a sense of deficiency, looked to make a name for himself. "I will be King." A similar statement made by Lucifer, and by Adam and Eve, and spoken by countless thousands through the years.

21. Refer to 1 Sam 8, NIV
22. Refer to Gen 3:14–15, NIV
23. Refer to Gen 3:16–19, NIV
24. Refer to Gen 1:27, NIV
25. Refer to 1 Kgs 1, NIV
26. Refer to 1 Kgs 1:5, NIV
27. Refer to 2 Sam 3:4, NIV
28. 1 Kgs 1:5, NKJV

Adonijah may have justified himself as he was a son of the King, and the King was showing signs of weakness both in his decision-making abilities and in his physical body.[29] This conclusion, no doubt reached by Adonijah as being heir-apparent, was incomplete and proved to be fatally flawed. Adonijah exhibited a sense of entitlement and followed the doomed pathway of self-promoting glory. He promoted himself and looked to others to validate his ambition "he made war-wagons and horsemen ready for himself, with fifty men to run in front of him."

This statement of validation would likely create a forceful means to bully himself to the throne and provide potent imagery of being a strong challenger to the throne, in contrast to his weakening father. This powerful image would provide the trigger for the hoped-for masses to join with his intent, an insightful glimpse into power struggles and the convictions of man. The story did not bode well for Adonijah. His attempts thwarted, his followers scattered,[30] and his life taken.[31]

Our deficiency can only be fulfilled through Jesus; anything outside of Jesus will never satisfy.

The story of life can be summarised as a longing for something to invest our expectations in. It would somehow appear that everything in life, that with which we experience, and that with which we desire, is intrinsically linked to expectation.

When expectations are not met, they become unfulfilled expectations.

We can find ourselves journeying from one experience to the next in search of perfect communion, and our inherent desire for perfect communion can have us enter physical relationships carrying expectations that can never be met by another human.

These attempts of meeting our need for perfect communion, through a human relationship, will result in our demanding that which cannot be delivered, placing the high demands and intricate cravings of our individualized needs on to another human. In all reality, this other person will also be on their search for completeness.

We demand too much from relationships when we desire a human to become the provider of the perfect relationship we crave, the perfect relationship that only God can fulfill.

We desire from humans more than humans can give.

The danger in placing expectations on an object or person is they cannot bridge the schism of the deficiency that we experience. The only way

---

29. Refer to 1 Kgs 1, NIV
30. Refer to 1 Kgs 1:49, NIV
31. Refer to 1 Kgs 2:13–25, NIV

to close this gap of expectation is to place our expectations (our hopes, our dreams, our desires) in Jesus. Jesus, as the only one who can fully deliver the life we so very desperately crave.

We have expectations because we are created for a significant purpose, and we want to know that our lives are making a difference during our fleeting presence on this globe.

The awkwardness between the genders as experienced through Adam and Eve is then repeated in our lives today. Adam and Eve initiated this awkwardness, and over the millennia, we have further developed this awkwardness, and through this, people are hurt and abused, belittled, and used.

Awkwardness becoming an unfilled expectation. Awkwardness growing to resentment, the breakdown of a relationship, and potentially divorce. It is the human desire for a connection that proves the fallacy of self-centric living and the need for a relationship with God.

Countless human relationships do prosper, and they do thrive, not just the ones where God is at the center of this relationship. A testament to the residues of love and goodness that continue to permeate through society. The tragedy remains, however, when these flourishing relationships fail to discover the source of their flourishing, and miss taking their relationship to greater heights. Alternatively, they may miss the opportunity of using their strong foundation to provide a caring platform for others to flourish. This is why human love is never a final destination.

Life is simple. Life should be simple. It is our actions that have made life hard. Jeremiah[32] speaks of two ways humans have messed up:

- we have given up on God as the provider of all we need; and,
- by abandoning God, we look elsewhere for our needed fulfillment, and by doing so, we only find brokenness

> My people have committed two sins: They have forsaken me, the spring of living water, and have dug their own cisterns, broken cisterns that cannot hold water.[33]

Separation from God is the root cause behind every conceivable issue and every real struggle we experience. Instead of returning to God as the source of our living water, we attempt multiple ways to counteract these deficiencies.

As identified just now, many humans are good, and truly stand by each other through sickness and health, through the good times and the bad

---

32. Refer to Jer 2:13, NIV
33. Jer 2:13, NIV

times, through times of need and times of plenty, they do this through the deposit of goodness found in each one of us. Others, unfortunately, become more desirous for that which can never be satisfied. We spend our lives reaching for the forbidden fruit and the forbidden thrill that comes through eating from another's vineyard. Perhaps, besides the example of Adam and Eve, King Solomon provides one of the most unfortunate examples of taking that which is forbidden and making these his own, from multiple wives to the building of shrines and the accumulation of unprecedented wealth. Later, we'll discuss how King Solomon epitomized poor decision making in contrast to the clarity of instruction that had been provided.

Alternatively, we are overcome with a profound sense of incompleteness that we look to numb this pain through passiveness or addiction.

Despite being perfect, Adam and Eve wrongly experienced a deficiency in their perfection. If we build our identity on our physical appearance, we have little chance of perfected character.

The human body is perhaps the most accessible form of comparison, as it is often the first representation of the person we encounter. And, it may be the only representation of a person we face when a body is displayed through media. We all do this. We see a person, and it is hard not to generate some form of comparison. We compare features and style. Modern society presents us with a constant flow of images depicting the perfect body, and this reinforces our vulnerability; either to lust or to compare. Social media becomes full of highly edited images of the human physique, and we can slavishly spend hours scrolling on social platforms comparing our lives and our bodies to that which is wrongly displayed as perfection.

Our faith teaches that physical features are of no importance when discussing identity, and this becomes of great relevance when reaching a generation that has placed significant value on the human form. The last human to see the face of God, or at least a physical representation of God in a way that we can understand, is the prophet Isaiah.[34] Additionally, we're informed Stephen saw the glory of God.[35]

Hence, we do not know what God looks like.

Jesus did take on the physical appearance as a human, but we have little evidence of what Jesus looked like. Some non-biblical accounts[36] of

---

34. Refer to Isa 6:1–3, NIV

35. Refer to Acts 7: 55–56, NIV

36. Articles discussing the appearance of Jesus. Article: The Ongoing Mystery of Jesus's Face: He is one of the most commonly painted figures in Western art. But what do we really know about his appearance? By Sarah Pruitt. Publication: History.com. 20th February 2019 (updated 2nd April 2020). Source: https://www.history.com/news/what-did-jesus-look-like; Article: The Real Face of Jesus: Advances in forensic science reveal

the physical appearance of Jesus are written, but the authenticity and accuracy of these accounts are debatable. The truth be known, we are unable to describe the physical appearance of Jesus. The Gospel writers choose not to include this, and we can confer from this non-inclusion that it was not a matter of importance for them to record how Jesus looked.

Despite the Bible offering no definitive account as to the physical appearance of Jesus, we have indicators. The Prophet Isaiah writes of the coming Jesus as having "no beauty or majesty to attract us to Him, nothing in His appearance that we should desire Him."[37] Can we conclude that Jesus was ordinary looking in appearance? Isaiah provides further imagery of Jesus's appearance on the cross:

> Just as there were many who were appalled at him—His appearance was so disfigured beyond that of any man and his form marred beyond human likeness.[38]

While this passage is prophesying the injustice and total cruelty to be experienced by Jesus, it does highlight how physical appearance has no reflection on his or our identity.

The Cross is described as Jesus's most significant work, achieved through the greatest sacrifice. This sacrifice was made through the brokenness of his body, in contrast to our desires to perfect the body.

Jesus's physical appearance had no impact on his identity. Likewise, our physical appearance does not affect our identity. It is the values and beliefs of flawed societies that would impose a sense of this not being the case. In saying this, however, many of us would agree to there being some type of connection between how we look and how we can feel about ourselves, and this self-perception usually generates from low self-worth, or, on the contrary, an elevated and at times idolized view of our physical appearance.

We do not have insight as to the physical features of Jesus, besides the glimpses provided by Isaiah; yet, people have developed corrupt philosophy based on Jesus's appearance.

The physical appearance of Jesus has been used to create systems that are in total contrast to everything Jesus stood for.

The Aryan race depicted the perfect human in the form of The Aryan Jesus. Caucasian. White skin. Blond hair. Blue eyes. Reality would be closer to dark skin, dark eyes, dark hair. Proponents of the Aryan race have used the comparison of the physical form as the benchmark and means to destroy

---

the most famous face in history. By Mike Fillon, Publication: Popular Mechanics, April 10, 2020. Source: https://www.popularmechanics.com/science/health/a234/1282186/)

37. Isa 53:2, NIV
38. Isa 52:14, NIV

those who do not compare to what they consider the pure human form, using Jesus as the center of this comparison. The ideology of Gobineau, Günther, Wagner, and Chamberlain[39] proved foundational in the racial policy and practice of Germany under Naziism. Using a false representation of Jesus to undermine the very reason Jesus came to earth: equality for humanity whereby all have equal access to God and whereby liberation is now available to all. Jesus came to perfect our identity and to lift all of humanity.

To use Jesus in such propaganda is the highest of injustices; such comparison did lead to the labeling of free people, and the stigmatization of entire races of people, and classes of people. Millions died as a result.

In a statement of absolute contrast to what would become the Aryan Jesus, Philippians[40] counter-outs any notion of Jesus seeking a discriminative position based on a physical comparison.

A person's education becomes another easy tool to create comparisons where most models of education are primarily based on a system of comparison. For every child living in a society where education is provided and whereby a child is legally required to participate, they are exposed to comparison from an early age. Children the world over can so very quickly become products of comparison, and society has established this.

We see comparison the world over. Protectionism, political extremism, nationalistic tendencies, narratives around migration routes, all being generated through fear-based comparisons.

Such comparisons do not lift. They only pull down.

---

39. See: https://en.wikipedia.org/wiki/Nazism
40. Refer to Phil 2:1–8, NIV

9

Falling Upwards

> *Eve:*
> *A thirst for status?*
> *A hunger for wisdom?*
> *A curiosity for mystery?*
> *A dare for seduction?*
> *A desire for transformation?*
> *A fascination with fantasy?*
> *A conquest for significance?*
> *A flirtation with experimentation?*
> *A want for something without the need for something?*
> *A gamble willing to die for?*
>
> —Nicholas Matthews[1]

DEFICIENCY AND TEMPTATION LOSE appeal when we consider and compare it against everything we already have. Similar to being offered a wreck-of-a-car when we have a garage full of immaculate cars, and this example comes no way close to what we have in Jesus.

I've often wondered as to the account of Adam and Eve's fall. They knew no life outside of perfection, and they lacked nothing, and sin was

---

1. Matthews, previously unpublished

perhaps not even a concept. I wonder if they had previously experienced any form of negative consequence? They were provided for, and they had each other without the relational strains of post-fall marriage. Yet, they chose to enter the forbidden.

I've often wondered as to the fall of Lucifer. Again, he was in perfection. Perfection[2] was all he knew until pride was found in him.[3] He, too, chose an alternative path.

I, too, wonder about my own life. I know the truth; Jesus has set me free. Purpose and significance are mine, and I still chase shadows, travel on round-a-bouts, and take dead-end streets.

The serpent appealed to Eve's curiosity with the enticement of falling upwards through the gaining of divine knowledge. The devastating reality, however, is that falling downwards is all the serpent could offer Eve. He'd fallen himself with no way back.[4]

In the physical, the serpent perhaps needed to look up to humans, and he must have realized humans were above his status as the "chosen ones"[5] in contrast to his state as the "fallen-one."[6] This reality would bring an eternity of torment. Upon Adam and Eve's fall, I wonder how the serpent perceived his position.

- Did he obtain the knowledge that his fate is sealed?
- Did he desire to get even with God, to get his own back by targeting his children?
- Did he foresee the possibility of God himself having to fall to earth to protect his children, and the battle fought in Heaven could continue on the future, killing fields of the earth?
- Did he crave subjects to populate his failing regime and to establish counterfeit heaven on earth?
- Did he want to wreck creation?
- Does he consider he is right?

The answers to these questions remain a mystery; what did happen, however, is the establishment of a counterfeit and terminally flawed regime,

---

2. Refer to Ezek 28:12,15 NIV
3. Refer to Ezek 28:15, 17, NIV
4. Refer to Isa 12: 13–15, Matt 25:41, 2 Pet 2:4, Jude 1:6, Rev 12:7–9, NIV
5. Refer to 1 Pet 2:9, NIV
6. Refer to Ezek 28:17, Isa 14:12–15, Luke 10:18, 2 Pet 2:4, Rev 12:9, NIV

and as the kingdom of God seemed to recede, the reach of this failed regime gained ground. The kingdom of dirt.

God would be coming to earth, not as a strong man but as a defenseless babe, and as the protagonist of the Genesis prophecy. The serpent was unable to attain the wisdom of God, and would most likely be in the dark of the Genesis 3:15 prophecy becoming his dreaded reality of John 3:16. That God would allow Jesus to be killed, reversing the curse of humanity's freefall with the invite for humanity to fall upwards.

In the one sense, Jesus fell upwards, and by doing so, he claimed the highest place[7] and modeled how we, too, are to fall upwards.

By being lifted, Jesus took the highest place.

There is no higher ground than the ground Jesus occupies. Everything created is positioned lower than Jesus.[8] Every knee shall bow, and there is no power on earth or in the heavens that come close to Jesus. Satan is not the opposite of Jesus. Jesus has no equal, and he has no opposite. Satan acts as a type of contrast, a comparison, if you will, to determine failure, ruin, and all that is wrong in this world.

Time does not warrant an investigation, besides the most fleeting of glances into the dynamics of the angelic nation, a nation residing within a different world, yet a nation whose actions penetrate our dimension, and whose operations affect our everyday lives. I include a few short paragraphs, however, to raise a point of considerable interest to progress this topic.

Unlike God, Satan is created and his existence, in a strange set of circumstances that one day may perhaps be revealed, only exists through the sovereignty of God. Satan is a living entity. Albeit, in the most twisted of versions.

While not encouraging investigation into the functions and characteristics of angels, the Bible does shed light on their role and shows evidence of differing categories:

- Seraphim.[9] Whose primary role appears to be the praise of God. Considered as the "fiery ones."[10]
- Cherubim.[11] Whose primary role appears to be that of guarding.[12]

---

7. Refer to Phil 2:9–11, NIV
8. Refer to Col 1: 15–19, NIV
9. Refer to Isa 6:2, 6 NIV
10. Seraphim being derived from the Hebrew word saraph, meaning "to burn." The Seraphim burn with a fiery passion for God.
11. Refer to Gen 3:24, 2 Samuel 22:11, NIV
12. Refer to Gen 3:24 NIV

- Archangel.[13] Amongst this category, we would consider Michael and Gabriel. Michael who appears to take on a warrior like existence,[14] and Gabriel,[15] considered in the role of messenger.[16]
- Angels. Of which there are multitudes. Daniel provides grounds for speculating the number of angels to be in the region of 100 million.[17] Be this a counted number or a symbolic number, representing an innumerable amount, is not essential. A third of angels are considered "fallen,"[18] and referred to as demons.[19]

Be they Seraphim, Cherubim, Archangel, or general angel; they share a commonality whereby they possess no self-sufficiency outside of God.[20] Yet—some or all, at one time or another, possess freewill within the sovereignty of God.

And within the parameters of freewill, a Cherub, named Lucifer, rallied an allegiance of angels in the rebellion of Heaven.[21]

And thus, the greatest of all wars, surpassing the wars of the twentieth century, ensued; a fight between two belligerents (Lucifer and Michael),[22] utilizing powers so violent that they impacted the universe and the earth[23] forever.

No human to human activity will ever match the destructiveness of this coup. Although the victory belongs to the King, the results of this battle brought sin to the universe and the earth, and its ramifications continue as do shockwaves reverberate once the initial earthquake falls silent. This war resulted in the eventual displacement of refugees (Adam and Eve) to a battle-scarred environment.

Lucifer leveraged his influence in the failed coup through the authority given him,[24] yet, within this authority, Lucifer, one could presume, knew he was no match for God.

13. Refer to 1 Thess 4:16, Jude 9, NIV
14. Refer to Daniel 10:13, Jude 9, Rev 12:7 NIV
15. Refer to Luke 1:19, 26 NIV
16. Refer to Luke 1:19 NIV
17. Refer to Daniel 7:10, NIV
18. Refer to Rev 12:3-4 NIV
19. Refer to Luke 9:1 NIV
20. Refer to Eph 1:19-23, Col 1:16 NIV
21. Refer to Rev 12:6-8 NIV
22. Refer to Rev 12:7-8 NIV
23. Refer to Rom 8:19-20 NIV

24. An interpretation of Luke 4:6-7 is of authority, domain, and power is given to Lucifer; by whom, the context and when is non-conclusive. In Luke, we do not see Jesus

Speaking speculatively, he may have considered God's most significant attributes (perfect love, generosity, and humility), becoming his greatest weakness in battle (passivity through pacifism, and the preservation of all life at all cost). Lucifer was deficient in understanding perfect love in the theatre of conflict. Not surprisingly, we too can misunderstand God's perfect love in light of battlefield ethics and morality of the Old Testament, and introspectively in considering the intimate battlefield of our minds when faced with destructive elements challenging our most sacred space.

I include this discussion on angels for just one reason; God has no equal. On the other hand, I consider Lucifer has a type of equal: Michael. Both created, and both have limiting powers within the context of God's sovereign rule.

Similar to Lucifer, we fell in humility. And through the victory of Jesus, unlike Lucifer, we are now lifted for eternity.

Falling upwards was now possible. It has become a matter of choice. Falling upwards in the secure name of Jesus would secure our identity.

One of Jesus's names is Lord.[25] Through the Old Testament, LORD, in uppercase, refers to God. Referenced hundreds of times, this name carries the most significance of reverence within the Hebrew language. It is the Hebrew name for God, the Tetragrammaton, transliterated in four letters; either YHWH (the origin of Yahweh) or JHVH (the source of Jehovah). "I am that I am."[26] Such is the reverence given to this name; the vowels were removed, deeming the name unutterable.

Through the New Testament, the title "Lord" as it relates to Jesus derives from the Greek word "Kurios," and this forms the shortest of credal affirmations: Jesus is Lord.[27] This short affirmation, however, has huge ramifications. In declaring Jesus as Lord the early followers faced potential death at the hands of the Roman Empire where there could be only one Lord, and this was not Jesus. Similarly, in declaring Jesus Lord would leave you in a place of vulnerability within the Jewish community.

The Bible will also use the title lord, in lowercase, to refer to a human position of authority.

Early in his ministry, Jesus asks the question:

---

correct Satan's claim to having authority, leading some to consider Satan was speaking the truth, while others, in considering the language of Satan is lies, lied. Should Satan possess power, domain, and authority, this remains restricted, limited in scope and temporal.

25. Refer to Acts 2:36, Acts 10:36, 1 Tim 6:15 NIV
26. Exod 3:14 KJV
27. Refer to 1 Cor 12:3, Rom 10:9, Phil 2:11, Rom 1:4 NIV

Why do you call me, 'Lord, Lord,' and do not do what I say?[28]

When we recognize Jesus Christ as Lord, our lives become forever changed. We align our lives in total obedience to Jesus. We acknowledge and confess that he is Lord.[29] This very recognition obtains our salvation.

Recognizing Jesus as Lord is a direct challenge to the idols seated on our high ground: some being active, some being passive.

---

28. Luke 6:46 NIV
29. Refer to Rom 10:9–10 NIV

10

The Challenge of Identity: The Front Line in the Battle of the Mind

I am no bird; and no net ensnares me: I am a free human being with an independent will.

Charlotte Brontë[1]

Lordship deals with the question of identity.

Our view of God impacts our view of self, especially self-identity. Until we allow Lordship into our lives, we will suffer, to one degree or another from a crisis of identity. If we do not know who God is, we will never fully understand ourselves and remain incomplete.

How we view God is crucial.

Because my identity is woven within God's reputation, it's paramount that my view of God is clear and without hurdles or obstacles. The agitator of our lives, the devil, has one aim and one purpose: to destroy God's reputation and to crush our identity.

There are several tactics the devil will use to achieve this outcome:

- Agitate our ability to doubt God
- Promote our ability to fear God inappropriately
- Advocate our sense of entitlement from God

1. Brontë, *Jane Eyre*

We do live unique lives, and we do encounter individual challenges as we develop our identity based on an understanding of God's reputation. Our view of God is the single most significant contributing factor to our ability to live fulfilling lives and to realize the full potential of our identity.

Our response to the Lordship of Jesus is in the choices we make. Ultimately, we have the power to choose life or to choose death.[2] This is real for the physical and the emotional where we have the choice to speak words that build up, or we speak words that tear down. To do what is good and upright or to do what is wrong and sinful. To live life in the fullness, or to live at differing levels of mediocracy with unresolved issues.

Living life in its fullest will require surrendering the high ground of our lives.

---

2. Refer to Deut 30:19, John 10:10 NIV

11

Identifying the High Ground

The most dangerous idol is our own selves when we want to occupy the place of God.

POPE FRANCIS[1]

THE HIGH GROUND IN a person's life is sacred, and it's invaluable that we determine how this space is used. We're created for this sacred space to be reserved for Jesus, but many do not welcome him. Or, after an initial welcome, we may dislodge Jesus through shifting priorities and alternative searches for fulfillment. Jesus will fight on our behalf and will defend us. It does seem, however, that he chooses not to defend his position when challenged personally. It's almost as though he voluntarily retreats in-light of distraction and competition.

Sacred space is unseen, and for this reason, it can go unnoticed. Years, decades, and lifetimes, may pass without consideration given to who or what occupies this space.

The Bible refers to anything other than Jesus occupying this space as idols.[2] With each idol bringing their own alternative narrative on the priorities of life. Idols can be people, philosophies, product, experience, or self-generated pride and sufficiency; anything elevated above God. The idols in our lives may remain silent, being effective in their ability to numb our need

---

1. Collazo and Rogak, *Pope Francis*
2. Refer to Isa 45:20, Isa 44:9–20, Jonah 2:8, Judg 10:14, Ps 16:4, Ps 135:15–18 NIV

for help. At times these idols may go unnoticed waiting for the opportune time to be triggered. Idols may cause toxic outbursts and advocate for destructive action. Often, they'll possess addictive characteristics; at times, they'll cause great unrest for us. Other times, they are rendering us lethargic.

Exodus[3] speaks of God being a jealous God. Not the type of jealousy we experience, but a comforting promise; God will not share a platform with that which will damage us. Just as any parent would not welcome dangerous elements to their child's environment.

The parent will do all they can to eradicate danger.

And this is the motivation for God's jealousy. Unlike the natural parent, however, God generally only acts on an invite. James asks the question, can freshwater and saltwater flow from the same source[4] and follows this question with observation as to the power of the tongue, of the considerable damage that can be done through such a small muscle. And as such, God will not share the high ground of our lives with the devil. However, he does choose to share this high ground with us, and this is through relationship. God will empower us to defend and strengthen the high ground in our lives from that which would destroy us.

The Bible sets forth a clear challenge; to not worship idols.[5] In our context, we may not necessarily consider that our fixation on a thing, anything, other than God as being an act of worship; it does, however, remain characteristically similar. It demands our attention, and often our resources, and we serve this demand through obedience. Within this context, many inadvertently worship social media. The ping of the phone grabs our attention, and we stop what we are doing to engage with the screen. We check the screen last thing at night and first thing in the morning. It may not be social media; it may be our careers, the need to be considered the intelligent one, the spiritual one, sporting one, or the fashionable one.

Quite possibly, money remains the most influential idol many will face. Not only the rich. People struggling with finances often elevate their fear and anxiety concerning their lack of funds, above God. Money carries god-like qualities, observed through its power over us, in its ability to impact us, and in its ability to become a craving or to cause a grave concern when there is a deficiency. It is the level of control and the level of its ability to impact our lives and to jeopardize our well-being that we do consider the reality of money and other areas as idols. Idols that gain positions of authority by climbing to the altar and high ground of our life.

---

3. Refer to Exod 20:5, 34:14 NIV
4. Refer to Jas 3:14 NIV
5. Refer to Isa 45:20, Isa 44:9–20, Jonah 2:8, Judg 10:14, Ps 16:4, Ps 135:15–18 NIV

12

Of Idols and Icons

Goliath didn't start off being 9' tall he started small; that's the same with all giants.

HEATHER ALDERSON[1]

RECENTLY, FRIENDS FROM THE Coptic and Catholic traditions introduced me to the concept of icons, particularly in their inherent difference to idols. I admit to previously giving little consideration to icons, but what I learned was remarkable. They taught how the concept of an icon merely represents something else and draws our gaze beyond and through the icon to see God. I researched further, and the difference is significant. Icons help our gaze focus on God. They act as a signpost to God. They do not demand attention, nor do they represent a thing to be in place of God; they require that our attention be focused and drawn to God. They are not to be worshipped, but they serve to be seen through and to reflect from.

An idol, on the other hand, demands attention and requires a position of elevation. It becomes an end in itself rather than a signpost. There is to be no further purpose beyond the idol. An idol requires us to pursue it, whereas an icon encourages us to see beyond it. The greed of money does not point towards a higher purpose than the illusion of satisfaction.

The ability to identify and deal with the idols of our lives is, therefore, of utmost urgency. It has the ability to propel us forward or to maintain

1. Alderson, *Empty Handed*

us in limbo. At worse, to fall backward. The ability to take ownership of what occupies the high ground of our lives is the transition from follower to disciple.

There is a marked difference between a follower of Jesus and a disciple. A follower of Jesus will be redeemed but may not necessarily follow with their whole heart. The disciple forsakes everything to follow with radical obedience and will experience the fullness of their liberation.

The tragedy of many lives, countless lives, is how they do not achieve their potential—bringing pain to the individual and God. Every parent wants the best for their child, and this is the case for God. He desperately wants the best for each of us. Many human parents would attest to the willingness to sacrifice their own lives for the sake of their children. This is what God has done.

The best way we can bring joy to God while rebelling against a sophisticated system based on comparison and greed is to live authentic God-centered lives. We are created to make Jesus Lord, and anything short of this will lead to differing levels of frustration and anxiety, while we write our growing list of missed opportunities.

It is possible to live a mediocre life, and it can be hard to climb out of this mediocracy. The world would conform each of us to primarily becoming an economic contributor possessing a pliable mind that can be shifted and shaped by the latest in thinking. Yet, the spirit of God lives in us, and perfection is possible to those who would choose. Human choice is a mystery, in that our creator created us with the ability to reject him.

A mystery we continue to grapple with.

We, humans, are rapidly taking on God-like qualities in our pursuit of creating robots and artificial intelligence. As far back as the 1940s, Asimov developed The Three Laws of Robotics.[2] Although premiered in the work of fiction, they have become principles to determine how we create artificial life. How do we created humans, create, and how do we then govern this non-human life? How will this new form of life (albeit artificial) interact with humans and interact with each other? Should they remain bound to the service of humans, or should they have the right to exist and determine their mission? The ethics of artificial intelligence is a vibrant discussion, and one that will only develop over the decades to come. If robots are to have rights, will these rights be their right to freedom of expression and thought, and any subsequent consequence through the legal system? Will

---

2. The Three Laws were introduced in Asimov's *Runaround* as included in the 1950 collection *I Robot*

they remain as robotic machines, or will they ultimately evolve to be sentient beings with the ability to perceive, feel, and experience subjectivity?

My thoughts on this are formed through the observation that human control, and our need to domineer as being kings of the mountain, will instill an unwillingness to jeopardize our un-God like controlling nature.

God valued freedom of choice to such a degree that he created us with freewill and provided the means to determine this freewill.

Making Jesus Lord of our lives is a matter of choice. Something, someone, or a combination will occupy the high ground of our life. This high ground will not be left vacated. It may be anxiety and fear, greed and lust, or a mix of attitudes and emotions. It may be a mindset of rebellious independence; "no one tells me what to do with my life," "I make my own way through this life," or rejected pity "I'm not good enough," "I'm too far gone," "I'm not worthy of being loved." We are unable to self-remove these areas, and we entirely rely on the Holy Spirit to do this, yet, it is achieved through partnership. The Holy Spirit will alert us and then patiently wait for us to ask for his help. This may be painful. It may mean confession, extending forgiveness, and accepting forgiveness, and will require coming to terms with a new style of life. However, this new life will be the best life we can live.

It can be said that to recognize Jesus as Lord, we first need to recognize deficiency in our lives, and to then recognize the need for a kinsman-redeemer. Should life be free of troubles, and we experience no sense of separation or isolation, we may miss the need for Jesus. Jesus is highlighted through our need and our deficiency, and it's often at a point of crisis that we reach for Jesus. A tension often precedes salvation. This, however, is not a rule as some would testify to their lives running well at the point of discovering Jesus. In these instances, Jesus becomes their purpose and completeness, their understanding, and it may only be through hindsight that the person realizes the definition of their lack as it compares to the discovery of their fullness.

God is all-powerful, and in his perfect wisdom, he created us with freewill.

The freedom to accept him.

The freedom to reject him.

The freedom to argue with him.

I once knew a man whose daughter had, unfortunately, made some regrettable life choices. He was a well-respected business leader of the highest regard and a beautiful example of a loving father. Through his broken heart, he would walk the streets at night in the places where many would tend to avoid just in the hope of finding his daughter. Night after night. His relentless love drove his relentless pursuit. I was a young and impressionable teenager at the time, and I consider how this story of a father loving his daughter demonstrated the type of God I could trust and the kind of God I could whole-heartedly advocate for. This story mirrors the father in the parable of the Prodigal Son;[3] in turn, reflecting the father heart of God towards each of us. The God Jesus came to highlight.

Similarly, in ways, to the daughter in the example above, there is a direct link between identity and kingdom inheritance. When the devil whispers in our ear or sectors of society do speak, "we're not good enough." When we believe this statement, we effectively minimize the fullness of our rightful inheritance due to the weakness of our character, and we trade freedom for bondage.

God created us with the fullness of freedom that would see the emotional breaking of our otherwise perfect hearts. The Apostle Paul writes how Jesus authentically empathizes with us because he endured every temptation known to humans,[4] and willingly chose the pathway that would emotionally break his heart through the rejection of those he created and those he loves with unconditional love.

Jesus was not married, but metaphorically, and spiritually we see the intimacy between God and Israel as a marriage. Hosea paints a tragic picture of the divorce between Israel and God. We wonder why God is so passionate about marriage; I consider it's because he's lived through the rejection, hurt, and humiliation of a divorce. He understands the pain of separation and has been left heartbroken.[5]

Larry Crabb expounds this notion of the marriage difficulties between God and humans:

> The Bible is a love story that begins with a divorce. Everything from the third chapter of Genesis through the end of Revelation is the story of a betrayed lover wooing us back into His arms so we can enjoy the love of family forever.[6]

---

3. Refer to Luke 15:11–33

4. Refer to Heb 4:15 NIV

5. The Bible uses narrative and illustrations describing God's relationship with Israel as two lovers. As husband and wife (Isa 54:5, Jer 31:32 NIV). Through the narrative and illustrations, the husband remains forever faithful while, on many occasions, the wife becomes unfaithful. This broke God's heart. The book of Hosea paints a vivid picture of this relationship; God instructs Hosea to marry a prostitute (Hos 1:2 NIV). Hosea's wife does not leave her former life and engages back in prostitution. God instructs Hosea to search for his wife and to pay for her freedom and to love her (Hos 3:1 NIV). Such is God's love for us.

6. Crabb, 66 *Love Letters*

Through our actions against Jesus, we rejected and conspired against him. Spat upon him. Tortured and killed him, and we added to the pain of spiritual divorce. We broke God's heart.

Through the pain of a broken heart, God authentically understands our fractured hearts. God knows this pain because he went through this pain and experiences this pain. He lives as one who has suffered a broken heart, and in his divine nature, he is the only one who can mend our broken heart. It is through our natural gravitation towards a healer; we recognize Jesus as Lord.

Making Jesus the Lord of our lives is a lifetime of discovery. So long as we continue walking forward, we are bettering our condition on a decision by decision basis. While young in faith we may be challenged to recognize Jesus in various situations and decisions. As we develop through prayer, worship, study, meeting, meditation, and contemplation, we soon realize Jesus is not hidden, we learn to open our eyes to see him and train our ears to hear him.

There will be times when our faith and resolve are tested, and we drop back, even slide back, but the Holy Spirit remains for each choice we make. For the new follower of Jesus, this may require stopping to ask Jesus multiple times a day for even the seemingly small things in our lives; activities and pursuits that have become habitual, or normalized, during our pre-Jesus life. In sexualized cultures, where objectification and beautification of the body are valued, how do we treat fantasy, coveting, and lust? To the enduring disciple, this is a battle where boundaries become known; for a new follower of Jesus, this may take many attempts to gauge how to navigate this new-found freedom. For the new follower of Jesus, the giving up of a lifestyle habit may be perceived as the removal of enjoyment and pleasure. The reality could not be further from this truth. God does not take away, or require abstinence through ritualized prohibition; instead, it is God's way of allowing us to experience life unhindered that enables us to engage life at a level the carnal nature has no match for.

Often, we will demand our rights and forfeit our freedom.

It remains vital that we can differentiate between freedom and rights. Freedom, in the spiritual sense, is freedom from sin. It is the removal of the constraints that hinder liberation; it is the removal of sin and the removal of death. It is having our identity placed within the identity of God. And it's in the level of accepting our freedom that our identities are shaped and become formed. Our self-worth and our self-identity are forged through the progression of spiritual formation in our lives. A gradual journeying towards perfection, requiring all the faculties of what makes a human a human developed in tandem with the empowerment of the Holy Spirit. The

Holy Spirit is forming and changing us from the inside out; the spiritual, the intellectual, and the emotional; so, we become whole to reach a hurting world.

Yet freedom on earth will not be realized in its fullness.

Rights, on the other hand, is a set of expectations we demand, usually at the exchange of a duty of compliance to established laws. When society demands differing rights, confusion can ensue. On a personal level, it's common to agree, the rights of one end where the rights of another begin.

The philosopher Zechariah Chafee encapsulates this notion with the following:

> Your right to swing your arms ends just where the other man's nose begins.[7]

The pursuit of rights will offer only a partial experience of freedom. Yet, within the context of this discussion, we do well to consider this is primarily focusing on spiritual rights. Human rights, or the rights of all humans to be loved, educated, protected, and determine the course of their natural lives, need our ongoing vigilance. As in the words of C. S. Lewis:

> There comes of course a degree of evil against which a protest will have to be made.[8]

Freedom in Jesus is not a demand for rights. Should Jesus give us our demanded rights instead of our freedom, our lives will be a pitiful shell of their potential.

Several years ago, I led a team of students to work in a refugee camp. The thousands of massed refugees were covered by a basic set of human rights, chiefly, the right of refuge. Yet, every face evidenced the fact; they were far from freedom.

Jesus came to bring freedom to the captive, freedom of unconditional love, and unconditional acceptance.

All we need is to be present. There is nothing we can bring, besides a contrite heart, that has any influence on this unconditional acceptance. The role of the contrite heart is of utmost importance.

In the modern world, contrite has become a little-used and almost obscure word. Yet, it is a valued life-principle to understand and apply. It's a word symbolizing the most important posture of the heart. Having a contrite heart speaks of an immense depth of remorse and recognition of doing wrong; it is being sorry, being apologetic to the degree that is hard to

---

7. Zechariah, *Freedom of Speech*
8. Lewis, *Reflections on the Psalms*

describe. It requires humility and acknowledgment. King David is known as having a contrite heart,[9] and a contrite heart is necessary for our spiritual development.

Our journeying, beyond the start line of salvation, is based on choice, including the option to accept liberation. Experiencing the fullness of liberation then becomes dependent on the choices that we make.

To walk with God, or to walk apart from God. These are the two ways to walk.

When we walk apart from God, we fall into sin and temptation, and ultimately look for something other than Jesus to occupy the high ground of our lives. These "somethings" represent the idols previously discussed. Idols that through empowerment, hold the ability to control or influence our minds and influence our choices. If left unattended, they possess the power to define our character and personality.

When we live apart from God, we start to justify our actions based on emotional and rational decision-making, and we fall prone to making unwise decisions. We begin to compromise God's standards by replacing God's kingdom values with worldly values and replacing kingdom culture with societal culture.

Inevitably, following God will include facing difficult choices as we learn to navigate away from self-reliance to a God-centric lifestyle. This requires trust and discipleship. Making Jesus Lord of our lives does not disempower us, nor does it take away the ability to make decisions. Instead, and through this relationship, we learn wisdom, and we are empowered to make decisions with higher results of significance. We see this exemplified time and time again, where God looks to the heart rather than qualification. Daniel is a prime example, rising from a defeated and enslaved nation to the heights of the Babylonian Empire, where he assumed the position of governor and prime minister. Joseph, another prime example, rising from the pit to becoming Egypt's governor during the time of Egypt's extent as a super empire.

When we walk with God, we posture our lives in alignment with the values and priorities of God.

Life in this flawed environment will create countless collisions between good and evil, right and wrong. In many ways, discipleship is a series of decisions that we navigate and respond to numerous times each day.

Researchers suggest we make upwards of 35,000 remotely conscious decisions daily,[10] and many of these decisions are based on comparison and

---

9. Refer to Ps 51:17 NIV
10. Krockow, *How Many Decisions*

prejudice through our systems of judging. We are created in the image of God, and part of this image is the ability to judge. Although the right judgment is a healthy and much-needed attribute in a broken society (the ability to judge safety from danger as an example), we remain broken people using a dangerous tool of judgment. Our response to many of these decisions will shape our future:

- To build or to tear down
- To serve or to be served
- To build an empire or to build community
- To be offended or to say sorry
- To heal or to harm
- To understand or to judge
- To build a wall or to build a bridge

Our response towards choice will have consequences for our immediate, future, and eternal lives.

Our choices matter.

Life can be considered, in its simplest form, the total of all the decisions and choices made. Some are influenced by the environments in which we live. Whereas the decisions made on our behalf during pregnancy, and after birth, are out of our sphere of control. But as we grow and develop, we will take on more responsibility for each choice and decision, through every stage of our life. As humans, we cannot turn from responsibility, and God has provided all we need to make the right decisions, and provided all the grace we need for when we act upon wrong choices. This provision comes through Jesus, who voluntarily took on our pain and hurt, and our rejection and rebellion, at the cross, the perfect reset-button.

Being creatures who possess the ability to reason for one choice over other choices does not negate the transformational role of the Holy Spirit. Through divine purpose and miracle, the Holy Spirit remedies our fallen state through supernatural intervention into our flawed natural circumstance. Personal healing. The breaking of addiction. Joy even through the pain. And purpose through discontent.

Pain can perhaps be described as the deepest of all human experience. When we engage this human experience, we search the innermost definition of that which makes us human. We cry for a healer, and it is this precise juncture that Jesus longs to be discovered. I've heard it said that an hour of pain could draw us closer to God than the reading of 1,000 books on theology. Nobody desires to suffer, yet suffering can bring us close to God.[11] The world would educate us otherwise.

Suffering, and the associated pain, will eventually cease, and we need a clear pathway to navigate ours, and others, suffering through the broken landscape of our fractured world. To align our thinking with the mind of Christ and overcome discrepancies that exist within our framework of understanding. If we are suffering, Jesus has promised to walk in unity with us. If we're not suffering, Jesus has obliged us to walk in accord with those who are suffering.

The Bible promises[12] that God can reach down to the deepest pit that we dig or the deepest pit others have pushed us in. Psalm 103, written by King David provides a depth of insight of forgiveness and provides a beautiful vision of God's love:

> Praise the Lord, my soul,
>   and forget not all his benefits—
> who forgives all your sins
>   and heals all your diseases,
> who redeems your life from the pit
>   and crowns you with love and compassion,
> who satisfies your desires with good things
>   so that your youth is renewed like the eagle's.
> The Lord is compassionate and gracious,
>   slow to anger, abounding in love.
> For as high as the heavens are above the earth,
>   so great is his love for those who fear him;
> as far as the east is from the west,
>   so far has he removed our transgressions from us.
> As a father has compassion on his children,
>   so the Lord has compassion on those who fear him;[13]

People, communities, societies, and nations will rise and fall based on their responsibilities towards their choices. We have tremendous freedom on this planet. Freedom that through rational minds makes little sense. Many agitators toward the Christian faith would paint Christianity as a grey lifestyle, controlled by the institution, with adherents stripped of pleasure, and who make choices that gladly discriminate. I fail to see this synopsis in the life of Jesus, and absolute freedom outside of God does not exist.

---

11. Refer to Matt 5:10–12; Rom 5:3–5; 2 Cor 1:3–4
12. Refer to Pss 40:2, 103:4, Eph 3:14–21
13. Ps 103:2–5, 8, 11–13 NIV

Jesus was a true radical in living out his intentional lifestyle. And this fundamental no compromise was pure genuineness, remaining truly authentic to all he was. In reflecting on his observations of the activities and practice of the church in light of Jesus's demonstration of vulnerability; Jesus's response to rejection, and his ability not to back down, Thompson writes:

> Christianity has struggled to occupy space in a way that mirrors the way Christ occupied space. Frequently, it has wanted to dominate space. Christ, in contrast, made space for others.[14]

The context of this essay was a questioning of when the established church, historically, reached for social and political power, a power that Jesus did not desire or entertain. The Gospel of John expounds upon this reluctance to earthly power:

> Jesus, knowing that they intended to come and make him king by force, withdrew again to a mountain by himself.[15]

The lust for power, even a passive flirtation with power, when outside of God's will is a constant challenge. Yet not the only problem.

There is a constant battle raging around us, over us, and in us.

Fr Raniero Cantalamessa[16] concludes:

> Our battle being against a triple alliance: the world ('the enemy around us'), the flesh ('the enemy within us'), and the devil ('the enemy above us').[17]

The good news remains that Jesus has won the battle, and we live as victors; however, the fullness of this victory, although achieved, is yet to be fully realized.

Despite not all battles being primarily spiritual, they can quickly turn spiritual through the impact they have on our lives as spiritual people. We are unable to isolate the effect of a broken bone on the rest of the body. The body will react. Nor can we separate the impact of an insulting word on the rest of our body. We will receive this insult and either forgive or allow the insult to shape our future self, and sense of worth. Should we forgive, our mind remains prone to remember. As integrated people, we cannot shield ourselves from such.

14. Thompson, *ABC Religion & Ethics*
15. John 6:15 NIV
16. Fr. Raniero Cantalamessa is a Catholic priest serving as the Preacher to the Papal Household since 1980
17. Gumbel, *Bible in One Year*

Be it sin, be it Satan, or be it the circumstances of life, we are impacted.

This battle may manifest in the simplest of doubts. A mindset belief that acts similarly to a dripping tap. At first, the drip is simply background noise, with very little notice given. After a time, this continuing drip takes a more prominent role in our life. It is no longer unnoticeable; nonetheless, it remains liveable. The busyness of days, with the interaction of tasks and relationships, serve to drown out this constant dripping. However, it remains. It is during the stillness of the night, often those early hours, those hours of 2 a.m. and 3 a.m., when the mind can become more alert that this constant drip transforms its ability to aggravate. It becomes elevated and jeopardizes our sleep and wellbeing, and at which point, takes a more prominent role in the everyday affairs of our life. It is in this instance that the mind may become an effective echo-chamber having the ability to reverberate and give prominence to the soundwaves of the drip.

Perhaps, the battle is grander and considered as a rushing and violent torrent of floodwater impacting every aspect of our life: our finances, our marriage, our health.

All the battles we face have their genesis, their origin, in the rebellion in Eden. However, not all battles are merely spiritual. The laws of nature do have a role to play. Cancer can impact the follower of Jesus as much as it can affect the non-follower of Jesus. A suspension bridge snaps and the laws of gravity see both the follower of Jesus and the non-follower of Jesus plunge. A city under unguided rocket attack sees no discrimination against the non-follower of Jesus and the follower of Jesus; both remain as likely to perish.

There are necessarily created natural and physical laws in play that provide the framework for living. Should I choose to jump from the Golden Gate bridge, I doubt that God would alter the laws of gravity to undermine my freewill. My choice to jump is a decision leading to catastrophic and immediate consequences. God's inaction in changing gravity secures the human race who need gravity to remain on earth. Yet, even in this scenario, God's heart would be broken over my predicament, and God does retain the right to intervene in the natural order of things supernaturally.

Some mechanisms do not discriminate. They indiscriminately target all. A concept Kushner conveys:

> Laws of nature do not make exceptions for nice people. A bullet has no conscience; neither does a malignant tumour or an automobile out of control. That is why good people get sick and get hurt as much as anyone.[18]

---

18. Kushner, *When Bad Things Happen*

OF IDOLS AND ICONS

Following this thought and within the context of the Sermon on the Mount sits a small sentence highlighting a broader concept:

> He causes his sun to rise on the evil and the good, and sends rain on the righteous and the unrighteous.[19]

We are all beneficiaries of God's blessings, in this instance, the blessings of natural rain. The good and the bad, the follower of Jesus and the non-follower of Jesus. Those unequivocally opposed to the idea of God and those discovering God for the first time. The challenge of Jesus is for us to do likewise. To follow the example of God and to be kind to our enemies.

Liberation from God does not mean, during our residence on this broken and corrupt world, freedom from the laws of nature. We take a hit, and we feel the pain. We fall down a flight of stairs and our bone breaks. Nor are we free from the negative complexities of human interaction. We project hostility, and we become lonely. We detach, and we achieve isolation.

The role of self, and our relationship to self, is a significant contributing factor to our discipleship journey. Discipleship requires a dying to; a dying to all that will undermine our efforts. When we fail to die to the demands of self, we, unfortunately, do empower ourselves and become enslaved to it. We see these different postures no better than in the lives of Jesus and Satan.

Jesus, who:

> Did not consider equality with God something to be used to his advantage
> Made himself nothing by taking the very nature of a servant
> Humbled himself
> Became obedient to death.[20]

Satan:

> You thought you were so handsome that it made your heart proud. You thought you were so glorious that it spoiled your wisdom.[21]

Isaiah provides five "I will" statements of Satan as a synopsis of this pride and his fall:

> I will ascend to heaven;
> I will raise my throne above the stars of God;

---

19. Matt 5:45 NIV
20. Phil 2:6–8, NIV, abridged
21. Ezek 28:17 NIRV

> I will sit enthroned on the mount of assembly, on the utmost heights of the sacred mountain.
> I will ascend above the tops of the clouds;
> I will make myself like the Most High.[22]

Later, in the gospels, Satan desires more than equality.[23] He wants to be the object of worship, worshipped not just by people or angels, but worshipped by Jesus.

The contrast could not be made more evident. Jesus, the name above all names, willingly humbling himself to become the lowest of the low and to die a criminal's death amongst the outcasts, and Satan, who declared his position to be higher than it ever was.

Pride was the mechanism of Satan's fall, and pride was now the tool Satan used to depose humanity from their place of status and to suffer his same fate. The fall of Lucifer, of Adam and Eve, and the continuing fall of the generations all attest to pride being the root of rebellion.

Pride is corruptive, and it works from the inside out. While remaining internal, it will manifest in self-serving thoughts, in thoughts that lead to negative discontentment, as thoughts that lead to jealousy, and jealousy resulting in the sense of entitlement. Such thoughts develop into attitudes, and it is these attitudes that can influence others and manifest as actions; the push for control, the placing of oneself at the center of attention, the need to always be right and to have the last word, and the need to seek affirmation.

Pride destroys individuals, marriages, families, communities, and nations.

Despite pride and the concept of self being intrinsically linked, the notion of self is not wrong. The role of self is essential to our transformation and therefore remains critical in our process of making Jesus Lord of our lives. A person can be saved but for transformation to not happen. It is possible to believe in the existence of God while continuing to live as though God has no claim over our life. This is a wasted opportunity to live the fullest that life has to offer.

Like Jesus, do we humbly submit? Or like Satan, do we proudly boast? Both options are possible, and both options are defining—one leading to perfection, the other, to enslavement.

---

22. Isa 14:13–14 NIV
23. Refer to Matt 4:8 NIV

13

Perfect

It seems to me there's an awful lot of trouble in the world that somehow wouldn't exist if all the people who sing such songs went and lived them out. I suppose I don't understand. But what would Jesus do? Is that what you mean by following His steps?

CHARLES SHELDON[1]

JESUS. OUR PERFECTION.

Being perfected is a heavenly gift where perfectionism is a human pursuit.

While perfectionism can achieve some results in the temporal, it's longevity and ability to solve the world's problems, and individual problems are limited. A perfectionist will take on issues without many options to unload. Perfectionism will also hamper excellence. The kingdom of God is excellence, and the person of Jesus is excellence manifested. I fear that the pursuit of perfectionism comes at a high cost, and this cost is the missed opportunity to become perfected.

Pursuing perfectionism will also require a process of validation as the perfectionist will need a validating system to gauge their progress. Perfectionists will generally become increasingly self-reliant and show little

---

1. Sheldon, *In His Steps*

welcome of external judgment or input. This self-reliance erects a barrier and can lead to anxiety, depression, and the life-style traits of a workaholic.

Human perfectionism is crippling.

Generally, it's a self-driven pursuit based on an individual's drive for a flawless outcome, based on their expectations. It is the striving for their desired future. Perfectionism is also a pursuit with potential and significant health-risks associated, such as anxiety and mental health. It's liberating when we come to the understanding that God does not require our perfection. He simply requires our joyful participation in his good and perfect ways. He knows we're not perfect, and he loves us regardless.

Perfectionism or being perfected.

In our ditching of the pursuit of perfectionism, we can experience being perfected while finding excellence. Perfectionism is a human-derived activity persuading our imperfect lives we can self-govern and self-determine a status of significance. Being perfected allows us to align our lives with the biblical challenge of "Whatever your hand finds to do, do it with all your might,"[2] where God gets the glory, and we share in the inheritance.

It can be argued that perfectionism as a team pursuit with altruistic outcomes can be for the good of society. Think researches and doctors striving for a medical breakthrough or a delicate rescue operation where one wrong move could bring disaster. In these instances, perfectionism can be in the positive. But generally speaking, pursuing perfectionism has the real potential of causing relational tension, be it the workplace, the marriage, the sports field, those points of connection where two or more people relate on a joint-task.

The disciples' life is based on openness and having a contrite heart. It is in knowing our limitations in the bigger picture of life. We cannot be perfect in our strength, and we desperately rely upon and fully acknowledge our absolute need for external help. We let our barriers down and welcome the flood of not only Jesus but also the human relationships that this type of vulnerability achieves.

Individualized, self-determined, perfectionism works in opposition to the intra-dependent, relationship-first, Christ centered life that we are called to.

We remain called to the journey of perfection without becoming driven by perfectionism. How should we marry the two? Perfect without being a perfectionist? This becomes accomplished through a relationship with the source of perfection; Jesus.

---

2. Eccl 9:10 NIV

Perfection is not an abstract or indeterminable goal; instead, perfection has a name. Jesus.

Jesus, the perfect one,[3] chooses, with absolute freedom, with the deepest of conviction and with the motivation of indescribable love, to reside in each of us, and our identity becomes perfected. Perfection dwelling in imperfection.

The flawless choosing the flawed. The flawed transformed to become flawesome.

Our bodies, while remaining flawed, will continue to act in ways far from being perfect, and transformation will continuously be required. This ongoing process of change and discipleship is the aligning of our attitudes, emotions, and desires to our new reality of being perfected through Jesus. A calibration, and an ongoing journey of recalibration.

It is being flawesome.

The process of transformation is more than change, a lifestyle add-on, or the assistance of support; it's a defining transformation at the deepest level. We have traded our sorrows and grief to become a child of God, where the God of the universe chooses to live inside of our broken, bruised and battered, deteriorating and dying body to bring life and life to the full.[4] It is God choosing to share a room with our emotions, thoughts, and to bring transformation from the inside out; for our new identity to shine through our human character. This is our defining moment in life.

The flawless in love with the flawed. A true romance.

God heals our wounds, restores our soul, and provides dignity and liberty. We become flawesome in this broken world with the promise of becoming flawless for eternity. Such is God's love for us.

We are redeemed but not yet perfected. A place of God's promises fulfilled and being fulfilled at the same time; this is how the Kingdom of God is already within[5] while following Jesus's instruction of praying "thy kingdom come."[6] It is our minds, our hearts, thoughts, our motives, our ethics, and our conduct that stands in the way of our perfected state. Our minds and our hearts will be fully and wholly redeemed, but they currently remain vulnerable to our broken society. This is where humility and repentance bring alignment to our lives.

We are in the current phase of being flawesome while living in a flawed system. Discipleship becomes our behavior. Salvation becomes our identity.

---

3. Refer to Heb 2:10, 5:9, 7:26, 28 NIV
4. Refer to John 10:10 NIV
5. Refer to Luke 17:20–21, NKJV
6. Refer to Matt 6:9–10 KJV

It's why we have spiritual gifts[7] and spiritual fruit[8] to help along the way. The Holy Spirit lives for this very purpose; to counsel, guide, and to empower our journey of discipleship.

The journey of discipleship is discovering the fullness of God and being radically transformed and aligned to God, who, by very nature, is the absolute definition of perfection. It is the aligning of our mind, body, and soul to reflect the values of the Kingdom of God. It is the manifestation of the Kingdom of God within our lives, impacting our emotions, our attitudes, our choices, and our priorities. It is recognizing Jesus as Lord, dying to self, and making Jesus Lord of our lives.

Dying to self can be a concept hard to digest. After all, our faith is one of life, and in the words of Jesus, not only life but "life to the fullest."[9] Therefore, we need to assume a positive to dying and a benefit to our involvement in such. Dying to self is a voluntary choice; to die to all that will hinder and harm us. It is a shedding, a getting rid-off, a stopping, ceasing. It is turning from that which will hurt us. Spurgeon writes:

> If you will not have death unto sin, you shall have sin unto death. There is no alternative. If you do not die to sin, you shall die for sin.[10]

Death through sacrifice is a common theme running through the Old Testament; in many ways, the sacrificial system formed the center of Jewish life and faith. From this period came the prophets who pronounced Jesus as the sacrificial lamb that was to come and take away the sin of the world.[11] Yet, to the hearer of the day, the sacrifice required death. Hundreds of years later, the New Testament introduced the concept of a living sacrifice.[12] A sacrifice that, in hindsight, does make sense. However, at the time it was first spoken, this image may well have caused a level of confusion. Up until this point, the sacrifice resulted in death. This new teaching promoted a new type of sacrifice that brought life. A living sacrifice.

It is an internal sacrifice allowing Christ to be formed within us.[13]

The point of salvation is the most radical transaction. Perfect, instantaneous, free, and unconditional. Discipleship, on the contrary, often looks

---

7. Refer to 1 Cor 12: 1–11 NIV
8. Refer to Gal 5:22–23 NIV
9. Refer to John 10:10 NIV
10. Spurgeon, *The Complete Works*
11. Refer to John 1:29 NIV
12. Refer to Rom 12:1 NIV
13. Refer to Rom 12:2, 2 Cor 3:18 NIV

messy, it will take a lifetime, often comes at a high cost, and is conditional. At that transactional moment of salvation, where transferral of the title-deed over our life moves from the power of darkness to the kingdom of God, Jesus will take up residence in our lives, and forever the perfection of Jesus will mark us. We call this transfer of ownership as "inviting Jesus into our heart."

Through this process, we receive God's good and perfect validation.

14

The Validating God

God saw everything that He had made, and behold, it was very good and He validated it completely.

THE BIBLE (AMP)[1]

WE ALL DO HAVE an internal craving to be validated by God based on his perfect love and our imperfect attempts at loving him back; God's validation of our lives provides the anchor and the security we need.

Needing validation is common. We need to know how we are doing, and we need to know how useful we are to society at large. Validation can make us feel good, but validation can also result in a negative view of life depending on who is giving the validation and the basis on which they are determining their feedback. Any validation generating fear, hopelessness, and inadequacy has its origin in the failed philosophies of the kingdom of dirt. While it does remain true that not all validation is welcome upon receipt; think of the student driver who has been validated on their driving test as not yet competent. Even when this validation comes from a need to protect and serve, it is in the positive.

In matters such as health and safety, medical professions, and transportation, we rely on a validation that meets industry standards. We expect a surgeon to receive validation through appropriate governing bodies. These

---

1. Gen 1:31 AMP

are functions validated, and this is good practice. Seeking validation at the identity level, however, can be dangerous.

When we consider that our identity does require validation, we can easily incorporate a Generation-Like syndrome. Who of us are competent to validate identity? The only one able to provide real validation of our identity is Jesus.

Of the most meaningful forms of validation given from one person to another is the use of their name within an honoring context, where the person authentically introduces and builds a narrative based on the person's identity. This provides for intimacy while developing a sense of confidence within the person.

15

The Importance of Names

A name pronounced is the recognition of the individual to whom it belongs. He who can pronounce my name aright, he can call me, and is entitled to my love and service.

HENRY DAVID THOREAU[1]

BEING NAMED GIVES IDENTITY and uniqueness. I have three names; my first name gives identity; my middle name is my father's name and speaks of legacy, while my surname provides inheritance. It is my surname that ties me to my wider family. I work with many cultures where the naming of a child carries great significance and generational symbolism while affirming heritage. These names, given in several cultures, also provide insight and knowledge as to their standing in society. There is usually a strong family link to names chosen.

Names are important.

Jesus carries the name above every name. The Bible tells that at the name of Jesus, every knee shall bow, and every tongue will confess the Lordship of Christ.[2] For people from highly individualized and independent cultures, this may pose an unwelcome image with negative connotations. Yet, in a way we do not fully comprehend on earth, we will willingly do this,

---

1. e-artnow, *Henry David Thoreau*
2. Refer to Rom 14:11, Phil 2:9–11 NIV

and in doing so, we discover the meaning of life, the fullness of life, and enjoy the most considerable depth of intimacy and relationship.

Jesus carries multiple names through the Bible. Many of these will be descriptive titles provided to help us learn of his nature and his character. Each title has specific relevance to his mission, his message, his purpose, his character, his nature, his attributes, his victory, his divine identity, and his glory. At those times we are lost, we can turn to Jesus our Shepherd,[3] for those times we are hurting we turn to Jesus our Healer,[4] the times we are facing anxiety we turn to Jesus the Prince of Peace.[5] For the times we face uncertainty Jesus is our Sure Foundation.[6] The times we need counsel, Jesus is our High Priest.[7] To discern our future, Jesus is The Way.[8] These names represent a select few in the names and titles of Jesus.

The more we study the names of Jesus, the more we can know and comprehend the fullness of Jesus, and the mystery of his being becomes apparent. Matthew, in the gospel, pays more attention to the name of Jesus than the events of his birth. Whereas John promises, "my Father will give you whatever you ask in my name."[9]

There is absolute power in the name of Jesus.

Jesus validated his disciples by calling them by their names. He knew them, and he knew their identity. The same being true for Lazarus,[10] for Zacchaeus.[11] The same being true for each of us.

Whereas God called Samuel through an audible voice, and Jesus called the disciples through a verbal call, God now calls us from the internal. Spirit to spirit. God not only calls us by name, but he also lives within the identity of our name. For the non-follower of Jesus, God continues to externally call by using their name until the door of their life is opened for God to enter and take up residence.[12]

When God affirms by using our name, we receive the greatest form of validation, and we are provided with the highest confidence to live by. We become validated by the creator of the universe. Many people fail to

---

3. Refer to John 10:11,14, NIV
4. Refer to Isa 53:5, Matt 8:16, Luke 9:11, 1 Pet 2:24 NIV
5. Refer to Isa 9:6 NIV
6. Refer to Isa 33:6, 1 Cor 10:4, 1 Pet 2:4–6 NIV
7. Refer to Heb 2:17, 4:14–16 NIV
8. Refer to John 14:6 NIV
9. John 16:23 NIV
10. Refer to John 11:43 NIV
11. Refer to Luke 19:5 NIV
12. Refer to Rev 3:20 NIV

hear God calling them by name, while others will misinterpret this calling as nonsense or folk-lore. Yet, if we learn to listen with hearts open, we will hear God calling us by our name, and our journey of discovering perfected identity begins. The discipleship journey of transformation from imperfect living commences.

We read in the Bible the story of Samuel as a young boy serving Eli.[13] God called Samuel by using his name three times. For the first two times that Samuel heard his name called, he assumed it to be Eli calling. God reached out for a third time, calling "Samuel, Samuel."[14] The narration informs:

> Now Samuel did not yet know the Lord.[15]

Before Samuel knew of God, God validated Samuel by calling his name.

Similarly, before the Prophet Jeremiah was born, we read how God knew his identity:

> Before I formed you in the womb I knew you,
> before you were born I set you apart;
> I appointed you as a prophet to the nations.[16]

In the opening narration of the Gospel of John, we read:

> And the Word was made flesh, and dwelt among us.[17]

The word dwelt (or dwelling) has linguistic proximity to the word tabernacle; alluding to a shared meaning:

> The Word became flesh and made his dwelling among us.[18]

Alternatively,

> And the Word became flesh, and did tabernacle among us.[19]

Whereas other translations use the word "residence":

> The Word became flesh and took up residence among us.[20]

---

13. Refer to 1 Sam 3 NIV
14. 1 Sam 3:10 NIV
15. 1 Sam 3:7 NIV
16. Jer 1:5 NIV
17. John 1:14 KJV
18. John 1:14 NIV
19. John 1:14 YLT
20. John 1:14 HCSB

Dwelled, tabernacled, and the concept of taking up residence would be familiar to the first readers of the gospels, words, and phrases rich in meaning and symbolism referencing the physical tabernacle[21] of the Old Testament, the portable place of God's dwelling and presence on earth; spanning a significant period of Jewish history from the Exodus through to the conquest of Canaan. Constructed, no doubt, by the wealth of Egypt carried away by Israel upon their liberation.

The tabernacle had the divine purpose of containing copies of heavenly things[22] and provided a physical representation of God's holiness and love contained within a structure that humans could grasp with some level of comprehension.

The tabernacle would require ongoing cleansing as it became like a bridge between heaven and earth. Contained within the tabernacle was the Ark of the Covenant, an elaborate gold-covered wooden chest, almost box-like. We do know that a box cannot contain God, but for this period of human life, this is all we could cope with.

Often static, but also moveable.

Other gods of the day were often territorial, and their territories marked by natural boundaries such as rivers. For Israel's God to be moveable across different frontiers and boundaries would speak with significant volume to the observers of the day; although God was represented in a box, he moves, and he has great and awesome power. For fascinating insight on the mobility and power of the Ark of the Covenant, investigate the impact of the Ark's capture on its new owners.[23]

The earthly tabernacle held humanity in a type of maintenance mode. Between the time of the tabernacle to the birth of Jesus, we went through cycles of loving God, to then forgetting God, to rebelling against God, to repentance before God, and only for the cycle to begin again. The sequence is most clarified through the period of the Judges. We, too, can experience this cycle in our own lives, often subtly.

But this was only a temporary fix and would become redundant once it became overshadowed by the arrival of the new tabernacle of Jesus,[24] the one referred to as The Word. The ushering in of the new tabernacle of Jesus enabled the new phase of our liberation.

Whereas the earthly tabernacle contained copies of heavenly things, Jesus came as the purity of Heaven to forever break down the barrier

---

21. Refer to Exod 36:8–39:43 NIV
22. Refer to Heb 9:23 NIV
23. Refer to 1 Sam 4–6 NIV
24. Refer to Heb 8–10 NIV

between God and humans. He was thus establishing the transition in the human story of God lovingly choosing to live in the hearts of everyone who would welcome him. God delights to reside in each of us as we continue the transformation to become the temple of the Holy Spirit.[25] The dwelling place of God on this earth.

Remarkable.

What we have is remarkable. I take this for granted all too many times. The temple was central to Jewish life, and the eventual destruction of the physical temple[26] would have been the type of loss I do not comprehend. It would be as though I awakened one morning and felt a dark and cold emptiness of the departure of God from my life.

In April 2019, the Notre-Dame Cathedral burned. Many of us would have watched the footage. For those not familiar with the role of the Notre-Dame Cathedral in French history, we perhaps missed the magnitude of this event. It was best explained to me in the simplest of terms: "the family home has burned to the ground." It contained their history, their collective identity, their family photo albums, the collective memory, and it contained what many consider to be the heart of the nation. It stood as a stalwart in the face of countless wars and occupations and has survived hundreds of years of societal, political, and economic change. As millions of Euro's poured into the rebuilding effort, the debate raged regarding how this money should rather be spent on the poor and the needy, and not in a building. Both sides of this argument were most likely legitimate in their position.

When a family home burns to the ground, there is little resentment, if any, when neighbors reach out and help. On the contrary, this coming together to rebuild a physical home strengthens relationships and deepens the community. I consider the nation of France needs to do both. They do need to restore what was at the center of their culture, while not neglecting their role as one of the world's wealthiest nations to meet the needs of others. Through this, a deepening sense of community can be realized. We see this time and time again in countries such as Australia and the US, as bush fires ravage communities, the nation responds, and community is built. Similarly, our natural lives can be restored after loss.

Since the inception of the human race, God's position towards us has always been love, pure love. For each time we mess up, individually and collectively, God meets us with a response of love. Our relationship with God bookends our human story. In Eden, and before the fall, we had an intimate relationship with God. We spoke to God; God spoke to us. We enjoyed each

---

25. Refer to 1 Cor 6:19–20 NIV
26. During the Siege of Jerusalem, 70 CE

other's company. When the sands of time do run out, and eternity for humans starts, the fullness and completeness of this intended intimacy will be restored. The space between the two bookends is our current situation.

Upon our falling, a spiritual veil was introduced to our existence, and God would become perceived as more mystery than intimate. With Eden closed,[27] heaven on earth seemed to recede as the consequence of sin and of having to work hard to break the ground, to plant, and to survive became the new norm. Nonetheless, a bridge between heaven and earth would be established; firstly, the tabernacle and the temple, secondly Jesus, and now through each of us as we become the bridge between heaven and earth. The kingdom of God is within. Within the hearts of the follower of Jesus.

The greatest privilege.

We have the kingdom of God living within; this separates us from the angels and elevates us to a position that we can only partially explain:

> nor will they say, 'See here!' or 'See there!' For indeed, the kingdom of God is within you.[28]

It is no longer an external physical structure that we travel to see; instead, it is a spiritual reality within. When we worship God, we are not as much reaching for external spiritual experiences; we are worshipping from the innermost parts of who we are. Our spirit yearning and reaching for connection with the one who loves us. We become, as it were, the continuance of the bridge connecting heaven and earth.

To the logical mind, this can appear absurd. Yet, the human mind is unable to fully comprehend the very thing that makes a human a human.[29] We could exist without love; indeed, love has little utilitarian use. If we are evolved animals, we can live, breed, function, and operate from instinct without the need for love. Love would be a detriment to our progress. Productive moments and years are wasted due to love. Broken love. Absence of love. Confusion over love.

Love can leave us paralyzed through the throes of first love, where we become obsessed with the concept and feeling of love rather than the person representing love. Our minds wander, and our plans commandeered around access to this love. Or, we fall out of love and feel lost. Or, we grow up with a deficit of love during our formative years, leaving us with a sense

---

27. Refer to Gen 3:23–24 NIV
28. Luke 17:21 NKJV
29. Refer to Deut 29:29, Eccl 3:11, Isa 55:8–9, Job 5:9, 11:7, Rom 11:33–34, 1 Cor 2:11, 16, Eph 3:17–21 NIV

of not belonging and of profound loneliness. Love generates hope, and a characteristic of Satan is to steal hope from us. In his intentions, he is no pick-pocket, taking change that we may never notice is missing. He desires the center of our lives, to place idols on the high grounds of our lives and to steal our hope.

What is more detrimental to the human than to steal their hope?

Our emotions and our spirit are attached to love, allowing us to love once a person has died. This is more than a retaining of memory and more than feeling a personal sense of loss. Love goes beyond memory alone. Love, on the one sense, does harbor our emotions. Love outlives our physical frame. Love does not die, it continues, and this is what makes us human.

Outside of God, love has no foundation for its existence.

God is love and not just a representation of love. God is pure love. Therefore, all love has its origin in God. As humans, we barely grasp at the edges of understanding this love.

My family and I had the privilege to spend some time with an indigenous community. It was a community that had discovered their place in the kingdom of God. Collectively, they were able to demonstrate this confidence. During one fire-side talk, an elder asked, "can a person who does not know Jesus experience love." It was a confronting question, not just in its simplicity, but also in its depth. The conversation developed while I pondered the question. My only input for the evening was a simple yes. Yes, it can. The closest demonstration of the love of God is observed at the birth of a child. A mother's love is beyond comprehension, and they would give their very life to save their child. A concept mirrored in the gospel story, a parent who would die for their child. This is love.

This level of human love, however, continues to remain incomplete. The fullness of human love remains muted while experienced on this fractured earth but fully realized upon entering heaven where even the very atmosphere of heaven, no doubt, will be the revealing of God as expressed through indescribable love.

God's indescribable love is often referred to as "light." Perhaps, best seen in the context of the Gospel of John:

> In the beginning was the Word, and the Word was with God, and the Word was God . . . In him was life, and that life was the light of all mankind. The light shines in the darkness, and the darkness has not overcome it.[30]

---

30. John 1:1, 4–5 NIV

In the creation story, we learn of how the light was a reality before the sun was created.[31] In the gospel of Matthew, we are told of how we carry a light inside of us. In heaven, we can expect a light so glorious that there is no need for the sun.[32] This is the light we carry within us:

> You are the light of the world. A town built on a hill cannot be hidden. Neither do people light a lamp and put it under a bowl. Instead they put it on its stand, and it gives light to everyone in the house. In the same way, let your light shine before others, that they may see your good deeds and glorify your Father in heaven.[33]

This light, and contrary to the popular children's song, is not little unless we keep it little; this light is the hope of the nations. This light is within me, and this light is within each of us. The kingdom of God is within. The kingdom of God within becomes the temporary bridge between heaven and earth. Between the fullness of Heaven and the physical frame of the person. This is how we can pray; your will be done on earth as it is in heaven.[34]

Jacobs ladder[35] alludes to this link, as do the occurrences of Christ, or Christ-like figures spending time on earth pre-dating the birth of Jesus; appearances referred to as Christophanies.[36]

The reader of the Old Testament, particularly relating to the function of the tabernacle, can experience a sense of wonderment and reservation, bordering on apprehension and fear. After all, the modern church is a far cry from what we read of in the Old Testament. However, these rituals and their practice were for our benefit.

The human condition after our falling was not able to exist within the proximity of the pure and unveiled presence of God. This would have broken God's heart.

Perhaps the best illustration to help consider this reality is that of a parent with a sick child in medical isolation. The parent can look through

---

31. Refer to Gen 1:3–5, 1:14–19 NIV
32. Refer to Isa 60:19, Rev 21:23, 22:5 NIV
33. Matt 5:14–16
34. Refer to Matt 6:10 NIV
35. Refer to Gen 28:10–17 NIV

36. Examples of potential appearances of Messiah pre-dating the New Testament– Melchizedek as an archetype Jesus, Jesus himself, or a physical manifestation of the Holy Spirit. The angel who wrestled with Jacob (Gen 32:24) is considered by many as Christ in bodily form. The mysterious man who appears to Joshua and identifies himself as the "the commander of the Lord's army," (Jos 5:14) is considered a manifestation of God. The fourth man in the furnace with Daniel is described in the following way "and the form of the fourth is like the Son of God" (Dan 3:25 NKJV).

the window, but to approach the one they love requires the donning of overalls and a face-mask so as not to pollute the environment, jeopardizing their child's survival. This would break the parent's heart, needing to interact with their child through the veil of medical gowns.

I've been in a position of needing to go through this similar procedure, not for one of my children, but a former student. The preparation I needed to go through to enter the environment of the room was thorough. And it was this thoroughness that prevented me from breathing germs or carrying particles on my regular clothing that could pose a contamination risk to the student. In many ways, this is a poor example, as this picture would see me (or the parent) in the position of God entering the environment of the earth carrying the potential of risk into the room. Yet, the example does fit well enough to use.

The formalized place of worship throughout the Old Testament was God's provision to connect heaven and earth without jeopardizing the occupants of earth. During our stay in the Garden of Eden, there was no need for a temple; we had the unveiled person of God with us. We now do not need a physical temple to hold God's presence on earth as he chooses to reside within us. We have the spirit of God alive and living inside of us, and we are now the collective temple of God. The residence of God on earth. Buildings allow us to gather and celebrate, and to pool resources for effective responses to the needs on our doorsteps and the needs across the border. Collectively meeting together provides an effective antidote to depression, isolation, and loneliness that is a growing concern in our ever-connected world. The temple of God becomes highly mobile, with each of us carrying the commission to take the light of God to all.

To ask the question, what form does this light have? We would conclude it looks a lot like love.

It propels us to live for the sake of others. It looks like reaching out to the harder places of the earth. It will look a look like not letting the sun go down while we remain in anger. It is the only way to live, at least, to live life in its fullest.

It is having the kingdom of God within, being the center of our life. It is the denying of all selfish ambition, every ambition that has a focal point outside of the purposes of God. It is the laying down of our plans and desires and realizing that these plans and desires are so very limiting. It realizes that God's plans and purposes for our lives are not a selfish demand given by an uncaring God; instead, they are intrinsically designed for the absolute betterment of our personal lives and society. It is altruistic and not loyalty, morality, or duty. God's love is the perfect example of altruism.

The flame keeping this light alive is made from hope. When we have no hope or little hope, we struggle to offer evidence of the powerful kingdom of God within.

The first years of the twentieth century saw the English Pre-Raphaelite artist William Homan Hunt paint his third version of "The Light of the World."[37] It is an excellent piece not only exhibiting the mastery of Hunt but depicts a remarkable story; a scene from the book of Revelation, "Here I am! I stand at the door and knock. If anyone hears my voice and opens the door, I will come in and eat with that person, and he with me."[38]

Hunt's piece is rich in symbolism, and central to this symbolism are the two lights. The light from the lantern representing human conscience, and the light that adorns the head of Jesus, representing salvation.

The painting depicts Jesus, lantern in hand, standing at the door. However, this is no ordinary door, it is a representation of our soul, of our heart. At first observation, the door looks weathered and overgrown with vines. On closer inspection, it becomes apparent that the door is missing a handle on the outside. Jesus is unable to enter and is obliged to wait.

Hunt's door represents our hearts, and the scene is of Jesus waiting to be invited in. Jesus does not impose himself, and he does not enter without our welcome. The door can only be opened by us and from our side of the door.

At times, we not only keep the door shut and Jesus on the outside, but we allow destructive options in. Temptation taps on the window, and we often seem keen to slide the window open and welcome temptation. Temptation is a destructive house guest who leaves their mark and mess scattered throughout. It trashes the furniture, eats the food, and leaves a pile of pots to be washed. The double tragedy of this scenario is the more embedded temptation becomes, the less keen we are to open the door to Jesus. Temptation will then open the window to the idols we are warned about.

All this time, Jesus is patiently waiting. Waiting with a broken heart and waiting night and day. For years, decades. Often, for the duration of a person's natural life. I was sharing my insight with a friend; we pondered the thought, could we imagine keeping a President, a famous football player, or a Nobel Peace Prize winner waiting outside? A foolish thought. Yet, we leave Jesus there.

There is a strange twist in the Exodus story where we meet Pharaoh in his resilience at the mercy of God. On several occasions, the Bible narrative

---

37. Refer to John 8:12 NIV
38. Rev 3:20 NIV

reveals how God hardens Pharaoh's heart.[39] This hardening of Pharaoh's heart[40] may seem to run contrary to Hunt's image of Jesus patiently waiting at the door. Was God good in the hardening of Pharaoh's heart? After all, who can resist God? Yet, a hard heart was all Pharaoh had to offer, and his hard heart was all God could use in the liberation story of Israel. God was liberating a nation, and the leader of a nation was standing in his way. Should Pharaoh have softened his heart and allowed his heart to turn toward God, the Exodus story could have provided a different ending. God knocked on Pharaoh's heart and was met, not just with silence, but with great defiance of injustice. A defiance leading to enslavement and suffering on an immense scale.

We may not be Pharaoh, but we can exhibit a similar hardness of heart.

The door to our hearts is opened from the inside. Jesus stands at the door to every heart with an invitation that knows of no discrimination. All are included. He patiently waits for years, for decades, lovingly knocking, patiently caring.

He waits as a doctor to heal our brokenness. He waits as a liberator to free us from our private prison. He waits as a guide to show us the way. He waits as a companion in our loneliness. He waits as a friend to sit quietly with. He waits as a conquering King to rid us of our demons.

The door represents our lives. We can hide behind our door, but we cannot hide the door. People see our façade, and they see the state of our door.

The human tragedy is we have many priorities knocking at our door, pushing to enter the heart of our lives.

Fear will knock.

Distraction will knock.

Pain will knock.

The strong will knock on the door of the weak.

The dominant will knock on the door of the vulnerable.

The marketeer will knock on the door of the discontent.

The remedy seller will knock on the door of the desperate.

So on and so forth.

Before long, we may find our hearts fully occupied, and this occupation soon becomes detrimental.

In opening the door to Jesus, we welcome him in. His mercy, his grace, his healing, and his love. In opening our whole lives to Jesus, we welcome

---

39. Refer to Exod 7:13–14, 7:22, 8:15, 19, 32, 9:7, 12, 34, 10:1, 20, 27, 11:10 NIV

40. My previous book, The Nine Veils, followed a conviction to discover God's goodness through some of the darker narratives of the Old Testament, and to use this discovery to discuss the goodness of God during similar experiences of our lives.

him to take the position as Lord of our lives. In making Jesus Lord, we permit him to rid our lives of the rubbish we have allowed to accumulate. As we walk through the dirt of a fallen world, we do pick this dirt up. Our bodies are immersed in the baptism of Jesus, but our feet require ongoing cleansing. Such is the life of the disciple. As the temple of the Old Testament needed ritualized cleansing, our lives today require similar cleansing.

As our lives are de-cluttered and the curtains opened, we give room for the unhindered flow of the Holy Spirit to permeate through every nook and cranny of our lives.

They say that sunlight is the greatest disinfectant, and there are significant parallels in the spiritual. By opening the door and inviting the sunlight of God to shine through us produces the most in-depth cleansing resulting in the most restorative remedy known to humanity, particularly in the broken areas of our minds where God calls us to renew our minds to reflect Jesus. This is not egocentric, on God's behalf, but a perfect example of altruism. Does it benefit God to have our minds renewed? Yes, in that he wants the best for us. But the renewing of our minds is ultimately for our benefit and the impact on society at large. In the words of Sanders:

> It should therefore be our supreme objective to have our minds so completely transformed that they will be an accurate reflection of the mind of Christ.[41]

Hunt's painting has impacted millions. It is a simple but powerful exhibit of the love of Jesus and has left the world a legacy to contemplate. In the words of Hunt:

> I painted the picture with what I thought, unworthy though I was, to be by Divine command, and not simply as a good Subject.[42]

The Light of the World hangs in St Paul's Cathedral, London.

I wrote earlier of the deep human desire for the need to be known and the need to be seen, and how these are two of the fundamental requirements for developing a healthy identity. Through the completed work of Jesus, and the infilling of the Holy Spirit, we are seen, and we are known. Jesus has gone before us, and now the Holy Spirit lives in us to reveal and validate our identity.[43]

---

41. Sanders, *A Spiritual Clinic*
42. St. Paul's Cathedral, *The Light of the World*
43. Refer to Rom 8:9, Heb 6:17–20 NIV

The type of intimacy our identity desires is met by the One who opts to "dwell amongst us."[44] God's preference would have been to dwell with us intimately and forever without the need of tabernacle, and this will become the preference for all of our eternity once we enter Heaven. On this side of heaven, we will continue to experience a deficiency in understanding God's love, and this is due to doubt and worry that retains the ability to rob us of the experience of the fullness of God's love.

God's validation of our lives becomes an essential reality in living our lives in fullness.

At the root of validation is the need to know who we are, connected with our identity. We need to know that we are valued, and we need to know that we are worth it. Our human constitution requires this validation. We need to know we are needed, and we need to know we have significance.

We seek validation. We need validation.

When we fail to receive this validation from God, we will look elsewhere, or resign ourselves to being of little value and low worth.

Reflecting on the conversation I had with Tin, as described at the outset of this book, what had become apparent is how we both identified the need for validation in our lives to counter the notion of insignificance and insecurity. But I ask, who told us this? Earlier in this book, we discussed the reality of having a deficit in our lives. Tin and I were validating ourselves. We were validating our perceived worth on a deficient basis of our limited understanding, particularly as it relates to how we considered others were viewing us. We both know we are complete, that we are whole while being perfected through Christ, but on this April night, we were focusing on validation outside of God's love, and we were listening with active engagement to a voice besides God's.

I'm involved in delivering training and assessment, and much of this training and assessment is accredited through a National Quality Framework. To evaluate against pre-determined standards of quality requires a review process, and at the core of this review process is the role of validation.

Much of our modern world operates on validation and assessment. Numbers are important to us, and we allow numbers to shape us. Who wins in sport is based on a number (generally, who has the highest number). Whether a business remains viable is based on a number (does the bottom line represent solvency). Whether nations go to war is based on a large and complex system of numbers (number of allies, number of assets in comparison, etc.). Who governs democracies (based on the number of votes).

---

44. Refer to Exod 29:45, 2 Cor 6:16, Rev 21:3 NIV

Who gains entry to university is predominantly the result of a number (the grading of High School education).

For validation to be attempted through social platforms, our number will become the number of likes we achieve. Seeking validation through social-media is becoming of great concern.

Without the foundation of knowing Jesus, we seek validation from many places, often to our detriment. Friends, family, and peers may offer productive validation but not complete validation. In seeking validation from others, we are asking the broken to validate the broken, where we become dependent on the changing heart-position of the validator. Should the validator be envious, jealous, or self-seeking, the validation may not be helpful and indeed can be hurtful. In the case of education and training, where skill, knowledge, and ability generate our validation, we can be left devastated through poor results, or, in other instances, our self-worth becomes elevated through validation.

Assessment is the foundation of this process of validation and becomes the means to determine whether competency in the areas of knowledge and skill is achieved. It's a judgment-based process requiring collecting and assessing, reviewing, and validating.

This validation is based on what a person can acquire and achieve rather than who the person is. Every student can be assessed, but not every student is validated as competent.

We can learn to take on the result of our validation, and this impacts our perceived worth and value. Validation becomes our barometer. We interpret the validation, and this causes our self-worth to rise or fall. This type of validation is based on shifting ground, where the tectonic plates of feelings and emotions impact the result. Validation, if done wrongly, can ruin a life. To our shame, and through our history, we have validated entire groups of people as of greater worth than others, leading to many horrendous outcomes. The shame remains as we continue to practice this validation of people groups.

When we turn to Jesus and make Jesus the Lord of our lives, we open ourselves to the validation of Jesus, a validation of total acceptance, total significance, and of our entire value. Jesus values our lives and accepts us for who we are, not what we have done or what we are to become. Jesus accepts us for who we are. Jesus's validation brings complete freedom and fullness of purpose.

16

How God Validates

Open up before God, keep nothing back;
he'll do whatever needs to be done:
He'll validate your life in the clear light of day
and stamp you with approval at high noon.

THE BIBLE (MSG)[1]

THE MOST CRITICAL VALIDATION in history was a universal statement made by God as recorded in Genesis:

> Then God said, "Let us make man in Our image, according to Our likeness...So God created man in His own image; He created him in the image of God; He created them male and female. God blessed them...God saw all that He had made, and it was very good.[2]

We are made in the image of God, and we are very good. God validated our significance.

When we rejected this validation, we separated ourselves from God. Even so, God continued his high validation of us by creating our redemption plan:

---

1. Ps 37:5–6 MSG
2. Gen 1:26–31 HCSB abridged

> I will put hostility between you and the woman, and between your seed and her seed. He will strike your head and you will strike his heel.[3]

Identifying validation in this passage may not have the same clarity as that of the previous passage; however, validation is at the very heart. This verse visualizes the struggle between the human family and our adversary (Satan) and points to Jesus (as one to be born into the human family) who will strike the head of Satan—God's redemption plan. God's plan for our liberation, where we see how God values our lives and how God validates us through redemption.

God so highly values us that he willingly sacrificed his son for us. The most exceptional example of human validation in its purest form.

God considers us worthy of redemption and lays this out in the gospel of John:

> For God so loved the world that he gave his one and only Son, that whoever believes in him shall not perish but have eternal life.[4]

Why would God validate?
He validates because we are significant[5]
He validates because we are valued[6]
He validates because we are of great worth[7]

We crave validation, and the entirety of the Bible reveals how and why God validates. Being made in his image, we bring God delight.[8] While in despair and darkness, God loves us.[9] God genuinely likes us, and he is on our side.[10] God has good plans for us.[11]

Whereas the world's validation is generally based on skills, knowledge, and attributes, the basis of God's validation is who he is and who we are. For the follower of Jesus, it becomes paramount that we increasingly discover who God is, who we are, and to gain a growing understanding of who we are in Jesus.

3. Gen 3:15 HCSB
4. John 3:16 NIV
5. Refer to Ps 139:13–16; Jer 29:11; Matt 10:31; John 3:16; Eph 2:4–9 NIV
6. Refer to Gen 3:15, Luke 15 NIV
7. Refer to John 3:16 NIV
8. Refer to Gen 1:31; Zeph 3:17 NIV
9. Refer to John 3:16 NIV
10. Refer to Rom 8:31 NIV
11. Refer to Jer 29:11 NIV

In my first book, The Nine Veils,[12] I identified and explored the link between God's reputation and personal identity, making the case that perfect identity comes from God, and how we view God has a direct impact on our identity. When we have a distorted view of God, we struggle with personal identity. To attain the fullness of identity, we need to have a clear view of God, and this is an unveiled view. The book identifies nine veils that are named and grouped into doubt-based veils, fear-based veils, and entitlement-based veils.

When we have an incomplete opinion of God, or we have the wrong view of God, this impacts our acceptance of his validation. When we do not know ourselves, we will struggle to receive his validation in our lives, and by default, we will look elsewhere for validation. It is in this looking elsewhere for validation that we see the seeds of distress sown.

Being sons and daughters of God is a predominant metaphor of our relationship with God.[13]

Petersen captures this validation beautifully:

> How blessed is God! And what a blessing he is! He's the Father of our Master, Jesus Christ, and takes us to the high places of blessing in him. Long before he laid down earth's foundations, he had us in mind, had settled on us as the focus of his love, to be made whole and holy by his love. Long, long ago he decided to adopt us into his family through Jesus Christ. (What pleasure he took in planning this!) He wanted us to enter into the celebration of his lavish gift-giving by the hand of his beloved Son?[14]

Validation from God is for our benefit, and God shares this validation to bring completeness to our lives. We are not orphans, mistakes, or tragedies, we are significantly valued, and God paid the highest price to validate us.

We all seek validation, and we've explored two sources of validation:

- Validation from God, and
- Validation from people.

The third source of validation, a twisted validation, would come from our adversary, the devil. It would be a hard task to find one who would intentionally seek validation from the devil. Nonetheless, there are sources of validation that reflect the priorities of the devil (hedonism, and

---

12. Matthews, The Nine Veils
13. Refer to Rom 8:14, 16, 2 Cor 6:18 NIV
14. Eph 1:3–6 MSG

philosophical Satanism, to name two) that will impact our sense of worth and well-being.

Should the validation we receive reflect the principles of life, to its fullest, we conclude this validation demonstrates the priorities of the Kingdom of God. Should the validation we receive reflect the principles of taking life, or the taking of the quality of life, then this would indicate the priorities of the failed regime of the devil. An example being the child who continually is told they are of no-good, and they will not achieve anything in life—the spouse made to feel inferior and controlled.

When we receive this type of external validation, we do have the right to accept or reject this validation. Yet, it is often through a complex and compromised framework of self-worth, values, and perception, that we may find ourselves inadequate to discern the negative qualities of this validation, or we become weakened to counter this negative validation from impacting our lives.

In the above case of the child told they are of no-good, and of little value, they will become impacted by the opinion of the person through whom this is being communicated. If this message is repeated to the child, through to their pre-teen and teen years, and through their young adult lives, they may struggle, and this negative validation becomes real to them. The young adult has now lived through an experience where their apparent weaknesses are fabricated. In the absence of their strengths elevated, this does provide fertile ground for low self-worth and low self-esteem to take root and grow. God can overcome this situation; should we invite him. He will validate our personhood rather than our character, actions, and behavior. Remember, "God saw everything that He had made, and behold, it was very good and He validated it completely."[15] You are worthy of being called "very good."

We need to accept this, to believe this, and to live this. Taking God's good validation of our life will require a shift in mindset, our mind will need to accept this. Our mind will need to overcome our often-habitual tendency to focus on our weaknesses rather than our strengths that do generate a toxic mix seeing us self-jeopardize our sense of value and worth. Through our relationship with Jesus, God validates each of us as being "righteous"; indeed, more than righteous, the "righteousness of God."[16]

We can reject ourselves or portions of ourselves, at least. We dislike a particular physical feature, or we compare with those we consider superior in sport or knowledge, employment, and opportunity. The key to

15. Gen 1:31 AMP
16. Refer to 2 Cor 5:21 NIV

overcoming this is through the total acceptance of the love of God to arise in our lives and replace fear with hope, rejection with love, and anxiety with purpose.

We need to agree with God's validation of our lives. God's salvation plan for our lives.

The point of salvation is where we accept Jesus. The journey of discipleship is where we increasingly accept the Lordship of Jesus over our lives. However, there remains the necessity of accepting ourselves as being righteous and of being perfected. This requires a rejection of much of what we hear from marketeers, and sectors of society, who would have us focus on our weaknesses to become motivated to purchase products and services or subscribe to particular systems that, by very nature, cannot define us or validate us.

The marketeers and social structures of the world will often look to define each of us by what we lack rather than what we possess. Validation is a need we all have, and the only source of true validation is from God who loves each of us for who we are, and this perfectly frames our lives based on who we are, and not what we are or what we lack. In God, there is no lack; there is just our growing discovery of God in his fullness. Our character remains under-construction, and God loves us through this process.

The principles of giving life or bringing death[17] represent two polar extremes of a continuum, and there will be much validation that occurs along this continuum. Some validation given is with good motives yet received as a negative; validation not spoken but involuntarily received—the case for Tin and me.

For Tin, insecurity was a self-diagnosed perception held as momentarily being true, a deficit of validation leading to doubt. Similarly, for me, I allowed this negative validation of insignificance to impact my identity.

We were exhibiting tendencies to allow this unspoken and invalid validation to produce doubt in our lives. We had mixed the clear validation of Jesus with our fears and doubts, and this provided a toxic message resulting in a deficit of validation, allowing doubt to enter our mindset. Thankfully, we both do have the maturity and discernment to be able to name this and deal with this. But for many, their deficits of validation can leave them stuck. Understanding God in his fullness is vital in the ongoing validation of our lives, and in our ability to live perfected through Jesus.

Our call to perfection is made possible through the perfect one, Jesus. His perfected work in our lives, promising a future of perfection while we travel on the journey of being perfected.

---

17. Refer to John 10:10 NIV

Flawesome. Our identity being perfect in Jesus, while our character remains in need of continuing alignment with Jesus through changes in our behavior. This is discipleship.

As previously discussed, John[18] describes Jesus as being the light of life and explains how we were lost in darkness. When light shines in the dark, it becomes visible to all who see. Jesus's life was a visible image of the invisible God.[19] God came to earth to show the way of perfection. Jesus exhibited perfection in character, providing the model of character-perfection. Paul, writing to the disciples in Philippi, describes the character of Jesus:

> In your relationships with one another, have the same mindset as Christ Jesus:
> Who, being in very nature God,
> > did not consider equality with God something to be used to his own advantage;
> rather, he made himself nothing
> > by taking the very nature of a servant,
> > being made in human likeness.
> And being found in appearance as a man,
> > he humbled himself
> > by becoming obedient to death—
> > even death on a cross![20]

Jesus has modeled character-perfection and has called us to reflect his character. A journey. A movement.

---

18. Refer to John 1:1–5 NIV
19. Refer to Col 1:15 NIV
20. Phil 2:5–8 NIV

17

The Journey of Discipleship is a Journey of Movement

> *Well, I always know what I want. And when you know what you want—you go toward it. Sometimes you go very fast, and sometimes only an inch a year. Perhaps you feel happier when you go fast. I don't know. I've forgotten the difference long ago, because it really doesn't matter, so long as you move.*
>
> Ayn Rand[1]

Jesus's first followers were described as belonging to "The Way";[2] followers on a journey, and this being a journey of realization rather than a destination. In life, we are generally running towards something (love, money, and experience, to name a few) or running away from something (responsibility, and our past as examples). We, as a human race, are dispositioned to move.

Humanity has always sought momentum. Adam and Eve sought the momentum of knowledge, and we continue with this strive for momentum. Indeed, the Gospel is a message of momentum. The disciple's call is to go to the ends of the earth for the sake of their faith.

---

1. Rand, *We the Living*
2. Acts 9:2 NIV

We push the barriers of technology to increase momentum; bicycles, cars, planes, space ships. It's as though we are hard-wired for movement.[3] At the bodily level, humans will pursue momentum for self-reward. At the societal level, we seek momentum for the betterment of the community.

As citizens of the kingdom of Heaven, our motivation is the furtherance of the kingdom reaching a needy world. The kingdom of Heaven does provide the answers to our common problems of healthcare, poverty, slavery, mental health, environmental issues, as well as every conceivable challenge humanity does face.

The follower of Jesus needs to align their lives to this ideal. Jesus taught us to pray, "thy kingdom come,"[4] and Jesus taught us to "seek first the Kingdom of God."[5] The responsibility we carry is to envision this kingdom and extend the frontiers of this kingdom to every hurting heart.

Several years ago, I became greatly influenced by a preacher speaking with great passion and conviction on the need to meet the hurting world where people are at. He said, "whatever we fail to achieve on-our-watch we leave as an inheritance for our children"; his context was on child slavery. His challenge; work towards a future where our children do not inherit the need to end child slavery because we have accomplished this, thus allowing and empowering our children to develop their lives without the need to tackle such problems. His quote was potentially inspired by President Ronald Reagan, who presided during a time of high suspicion between rival super-powers and their alliances. A time where humanity had amassed enough knowledge to end their occupancy on God's earth:

> Our moral imperative is to work with all powers for that day when the children of the world will grow up without the fear of nuclear war.[6]

And looking forward, we have a brighter future awaiting us. Not limited to a temporary cessation of hostility between families and nations, but an absolute termination of resentment, for eternity, where the curse of sin is removed. And with this, the end of temptation and lust, to be replaced with an alternative far superior to anything the mind can currently fantasize.

The kingdom of God will ultimately restore creation to God's original intent; summarised beautifully in the books of Isaiah and Revelation:

Firstly, Isaiah:

---

3. Refer to Phil 1:22–25 NIV
4. Matt 6:10 KJV
5. Matt 6:33 NIV
6. Anderson and Anderson, *Reagan's Secret War*

> The wolf will live with the lamb,
> the leopard will lie down with the goat,
> The cow will feed with the bear,
> The infant will play near the cobra's den,
> They will neither harm nor destroy.[7]

And secondly, Revelation:

> Then I saw "a new heaven and a new earth," for the first heaven and the first earth had passed away . . . And I heard a loud voice from the throne saying, "Look! God's dwelling place is now among the people, and he will dwell with them. They will be his people, and God himself will be with them and be their God. 'He will wipe every tear from their eyes. There will be no more death' or mourning or crying or pain, for the old order of things has passed away.[8]

Exploration and discovery are natural for us, and freedom of movement is enshrined as a human right. Any attempt to limit human movement is often met with protests and outcry. Totalitarian governments will push against this and actively block or limit this freedom of movement.

Yet, spiritual movement, a movement towards the ideal of Jesus, outweighs our physical movement. Nonetheless, the perfecting of our spiritual journey may well provide the opportunity to physically move through this world as we respond to the good news of Jesus.

The Bible is a book of a journey. We are given little detail on the final destination, and we are given little insight before Adam and Eve, but we are given all that we need to succeed in this journey of life.

Central to Jesus's teaching, and described as amongst the greatest of speeches (Gandhi and Tolstoy, to name a few) is the Sermon on the Mount. The Sermon reveals how to live and how to align our spiritual nature to God. It shows the priorities of God and builds a foundation from which our identity is secured. It is the simplest of messages that every human from every culture and background can fulfill. It teaches ethics and morals while presenting a code of conduct, and a challenge to act from the love of God.

The sermon builds on sayings and teaching of Jesus describing how to be people of the kingdom of Heaven; thus, it becomes essential reading for the follower of Jesus. It describes the character of the people of the kingdom of Heaven. A character defined by the ideal of love and humility, the

---

7. Isa 11:6–9 NIV abridged
8. Rev 21: 1, 3–4 NIV

THE JOURNEY OF DISCIPLESHIP IS A JOURNEY OF MOVEMENT 95

importance of spirituality, and the necessity of compassion. It constitutes a movement from independence and self-centric living to community.

The sermon carries a direct challenge "Be perfect, therefore, as your heavenly Father is perfect."[9] Being perfect, therefore, is both achievable and remains a requirement not based on competence; instead, a need that is based on validation, God's validation of each of our lives. Within this sermon, Jesus validates us by calling us "the salt of the earth"[10] and the "light of the world"[11] where God entrusts us to shine on his behalf.

This call to perfection is to seek the path leading to perfection found within the Kingdom of Heaven. We journey in the direction of perfection from the place of being perfected; arrived yet still journeying.

The sermon does not downplay the hard conditions that humans can find themselves in. It is the realization that the Christian life is not complicated; it is, nonetheless, hard. It is written to various circumstances; those who are thirsty, those who are hungry. Those who have come to the end of themselves, those who have sorrow, those for whom life is just plain hard. Jesus comforts them by saying, The Kingdom of God belongs to them, and within the Kingdom of God, they will find comfort and happiness. The sermon contains promises that the riches of heaven and earth, being filled and seeing God, and being called Sons of God, will be theirs.

The sermon sheds light on motives and identity. It contrasts the actions of those who would perform for recognition by seeking glory in the eyes of fellow humans through a superficial attempt at spirituality, with those who seek first the kingdom of God and who would labor on behalf of others simply because of God's love, driven by a heart motivation.

Jesus knows the importance of living from authentic identity, and he speaks:

> Be careful not to practice your righteousness in front of others to be seen by them.[12]
> Do not be as those who pretend to be someone they are not.[13]
> Do not be like them.[14]
> You who pretend to be someone you are not.[15]

---

9. Matt 5:48 NIV
10. Matt 5:13 NIV
11. Matt 5:14–16 NIV
12. Matt 6:1 NIV
13. Matt 6:2 NLV
14. Matt 6:8 NIV
15. Matt 7:5 NLV

The world tends to determine what is fake and what is authentic. And Jesus's sermon puts the onus on the reader to live authentically. The difference between "acting" and "being." Acting will tire us, is unsustainable, and is seen as unauthentic. Being, on the other hand, is authentic, brings inner peace, and leads to perfection.

18

Being Perfect

Certain new theologians dispute original sin, which is the only part of Christian theology which can really be proved.

G. K. Chesterton[1]

AT THE OUTSET OF this book, I presented several principles that provide the foundational theory of this book. Four of these principles relate directly to perfection:

- God is the definition of perfection, referred to within the Bible as being Awesome. We are perfected through Jesus while being perfected through the work of the Holy Spirit
- We are responsible, through the Holy Spirit, for the renewing of our minds and the transformation of our lives
- We can wrongly assume our flawed character defines our identity
- Our ancestors rejected perfect living in Eden and initiated a fractured and flawed existence. We now navigate this reality

These principles can create a paradoxical situation where our lives continue to exhibit the flawed principles of the world, while at the same time, having already become perfected. It is almost as though we have competing narratives in our lives. To some degree, this is true.

1. Ahlquist, *G. K. Chesterton*

This dynamic can leave us feeling imperfect. We can view the reflection in the mirror and see the imperfection behind the face. Our flawed societies influence us, and we can act imperfectly. The unfortunate reality for many, however, is to be defined by flawed character rather than by perfected identity, and we wrongly assume that our flawed character is an outward expression of our inevitable flawed identity.

Thankfully, this is not who we are.

Our identity is as a beloved child of the King. Within God's kingdom, there is no class system, no disadvantage, and no favored status. Luke, in the book of Acts, writes:

> Then Peter opened his mouth, and said, Of a truth I perceive that God is no respecter of persons.[2]

A theme repeated by Paul in the book of Romans:

> For God does not show favouritism.[3]

God does not forget us or ignore us. There is no discrimination, and we will never be downtrodden. In contrast, we are seen, valued, and we are known.

The paradox, therefore, becomes a non-paradox.

God provides all that we need, and he offers this through a sure foundation securing and anchoring our lives. A perfect you in an imperfect you. We are redeemed and in the process of redemption. Purified and in the process of cleansing. And we are sanctified while in the process of sanctification. This is who we are.

Through life, we will mirror our priorities, and we will respond through the positioning of our hearts. When our priority is for the kingdom of Heaven, this positioning will be evidenced in our lives. When our preference is for secular advancement, we will, in turn, reflect these values. Some days we will stumble, but we will never lose our identity as being perfected through Jesus.

The challenge remains when our character behaves poorly in the view of a watching world. Accusations of hypocrisy are directed towards those who believe in Jesus, and therefore the need to be transparent and open, being quick to seek forgiveness and to acknowledge our poor choice is of vital concern to the follower of Jesus.

Only one human has ever lived perfectly, and the world's judgment may diminish in the face of a sincere and apologetic heart. We are broken

---

2. Acts 10:34, KJV
3. Rom 2:11 NIV

vessels to one extent or the other. Yet, it is often through our cracks that the light of Jesus shines out.

It remains true that the follower of Jesus can agitate, irritate, neglect, and inflame to the detriment of relationships, yet, we have all we need to make every choice, and every relationship prosper and succeed. The spirit of God is deposited in our lives for this purpose, and we have the authenticity and availability of these blessings to navigate life (Love. Joy. Peace. Patience. Kindness. Goodness. Faithfulness. Gentleness. Self-control).[4]

The concept of the perfect you (identity) and the imperfect you (character) sharing the same physical frame produces an internal battle.

---

4. Refer to Gal 5:22–23 ESV

19

The Battle for Identity

Penetrate, at certain hours, past the livid face of a human being who is engaged in reflection, and look behind, gaze into that soul, gaze into that obscurity. There, beneath that external silence, battles of giants, like those recorded in Homer, are in progress; skirmishes of dragons and hydras and swarms of phantoms, as in Milton; visionary circles, as in Dante.

Victor Hugo[1]

Our God-given identity is the most precious gift. It validates who we are, and it validates our purpose.

The first recorded question asked by God to humanity is a direct question reaching to the identity of the recipients: "Where are you?" The purpose of this question was not for God to gain information, for God knew their location. He was concerned with their identity.

It was a leading question aimed at the heart of the problem. "Where are you?"; speaking of a state-of-mind rather than a geographic location. It is a deep call to the innermost parts of the human constitution, a question relating to identity. Where are you? It's a question showing how God cares. He cares about what we are involved with. It's a question revealing how God is interested in each of us, and evidence enough that God speaks.

---

1. Hugo, *Les Misérables*

Eve, preceding God's question, was confronted with an earlier question. This question, asked by the serpent,[2] was an attack at the heart of Eve's identity, and it was a question that generated doubt. "Are you sure?" asked the serpent, and the seeds of doubt took root in Eve's identity and later, in our collective identity. Doubt robbed Adam and Eve while doubt continues to rob us, their descendants. The perfected work of Jesus removes doubt from our identity; yet, doubts remain in our minds.

We do see how quickly doubt had germinated in the life of Eve, for just as soon as the first seed of doubt was sown, the first fruit of this doubt developed into accusatory questioning. Eve added her voice to this doubt by internally questioning God's best intentions.[3] Questioning is often the right thing to do, and we do need to ask to navigate and develop. The motivation of the questioner, however, becomes vital in recognizing the position of the questioners' heart. Is the question generated from an eagerness to learn, or the desire to accuse?

Already knowing the answer, God is leading in with a question to draw a response from Adam and Eve, and to build towards a better future.

What we can be sure of; this question was for the benefit of Adam and Eve, and our benefit also. We know this question was one of great significance and importance, and it would take an internal examination, openness, and humility to provide an answer reflecting the circumstances.

God's question to Adam and Eve is as relevant today in each of our lives as it was to Adam and Eve thousands of years ago.

God still asks, "Where are we?"
In our life?
In our dreams?
In our relationships?
In our health?

"Where are we?"
Spiritually?
Emotionally?
Psychologically?
Physically?

"Where are we?"
In our challenges?
In our careers?

2. Refer to Gen 3:1 NIV
3. Refer to Gen 3:6 NIV

In our goals?

In our education?

Do we know where we are? Do we know where we are going? Do we know what is happening? Where's our current focus? These are the right questions to ask.

The importance of these questions highlights how we are unable to self-govern to the degree whereby we discern the purpose and meaning of life. We are not able to insulate against the challenges that will undermine us. Nor are we able to rejection-proof our lives.

We do remain fractured, and we do stay in need of help.

Two related questions need to be asked: "where are you from?" and "where are you going." The first relating to inheritance and the latter relating to legacy. Where did you start, and where will you finish? Gauging our progress against, and our response to these two questions will provide insight as to benchmark our journey.

I come from a culture where it's common to say, not to ask, but to say, "how are you?" without expecting an answer that accurately reflects their circumstances. It's an etiquette exchange, and the hearer generally understands that if the conditions are appropriate for a real answer to be given, then a more in-depth conversation can entail. This exchange between friends, a question relating to the depths of identity ("how are you?") is often asked and answered at a very surface level, where it is enough to say "fine" even when we are not. Is this simply a cultural norm? Avoidance at the emotional level? A display of people who do not want to be probed and people who do not wish to probe? In many ways, God's question sets a precedent for all of us. It is the first recorded question from God in our history, and it goes to the heart of our identity.

Society, at large, is starting to take the issue of mental health to a more severe level. Taboos surrounding mental health are being dismantled, and house-hold names are finding the courage to stand up and tell their story of mental health. Australia and many countries are promoting the use of "R U OK." Four simple letters, representing issues in the deepest parts of our lives. Four letters we are being encouraged to ask each other. Similar to God's investigation of Adam and Eve, he was asking, are you okay?

20

Defining Identity

Every ant knows the formula of its ant-hill,
every bee knows the formula of its beehive.
They know it in their own way, not in our way.
Only humankind does not know its own formula.

FYODOR DOSTOEVSKY[1]

THE QUESTION OF HUMAN identity is understood through various disciplines. Through the social sciences, identity describes the person's comprehension of themselves. While in philosophy, the definition would consider the things that make a person a person. Psychology would develop this definition of identity by incorporating the person's personality, their beliefs, their qualities, and their expression of such.

There are other contributing factors shaping personal identity. At the micro-level, we self-define. Whereas, at the meso-level, our identity is defined by those who view us, predominantly our local communities and nuclear families. From a broader approach, identity has a more socially construed element where identities form through a more considerable macro-level societal involvement—leading to a global-level identity with global perspectives and trends somewhat defining our identity.

1. Dostoevsky, as quoted on Goodreads

Through life, we will identify with many things—political persuasion, economic viewpoint, a sports team, affiliation, or to define through a genre. We also identify through belief and religion, and within our faith, we can identify through association with a style of worship demonstrated. For the follower of Jesus, our identity comes not from within nor from the world; rather, it comes from God.

God does create humans as individuals, but he places us in the community, and for relationship. The primary source of identity for the follower of Jesus is identification with God. When our identification with God is hindered, we feel this through perceived deficiencies in our identity. It is this spiritual condition that widens our definition of personal identity. We are not insular human beings. We are not as robots unable to hold the individual capacity to be creative with a unique personality. Instead, it gives confidence in our very foundation. We have a solid rock, a sure foundation to live.

Our identity is found in God. It's not an individualistic human trait, but a connected spiritual reality.

As a newborn, we may have limited discernment of our identity. As we grow, we grow in recognition of our identity, and our persona will reflect our understanding of this. Indeed, even through to our latter years, we continue the journey of discovering who we are. I do not doubt that we will continue to surprise ourselves until our dying day. Unlike the ant in Dostoevsky's quote, we often do remain perplexed as to who we are. Therefore, the fullness of identity is discovered through the one who knows us well.

A review of the Bible generates a wealth of definition as to our identity.

21

The Human Condition

The mind of man is a battleground on which every moral and spiritual battle is fought. Because of its inherited bias toward sin, the natural mind is hostile to God and does not submit to God's law—"indeed, it cannot."

OSWALD SANDERS[1]

WE OFTEN DEMONSTRATE A collective hostility toward God, and this is the crux of our collective responsibility for the state of our human race and our planet.

There is a concept referred to as total depravity, and this total depravity defines the human condition; we are members of a fallen species, and this state of total depravity, unfortunately, produces who we are.

In 1958, Sanders addressed the fallen nature of humanity and, in using select words, wrote of our life as having a "fatal disability,"[2] and having a "bias towards sin."[3]

The Bible is evident in its telling of the fallen state of human nature. It describes the impact of the fall on the first of our kind, and how we needed intervention and liberty at the deepest level. The fall, however, paved the

1. Sanders, *A Spiritual Clinic*
2. Sanders, *A Spiritual Clinic*
3. Sanders, *A Spiritual Clinic*

way for future hope and liberation. Through Jesus, our condition is in the process of restoration back to its original condition. Yet, there was to be a heavy price to restore humanity.

Jesus became kinsman-redeemer for our fallen race. Whereas depravity entered through the man Adam, redemption came through the man Jesus. In becoming our second Adam,[4] the second man born without a sinful nature,[5] Jesus became one of us, to pay the price for our redemption. It took a full human to redeem the whole human race.

Total depravity is not easy reading, yet provides insight as to the dramatic change in our human condition since the fall at Eden. We lost perfection, and we became flawed. We lost innocence, and we gained the knowledge to be able to project evil through the generations to come. Through Adam and Eve's selection of what was forbidden, our human condition became utterly and eternally flawed. We became a flawed race living in a perfect environment (the Garden of Eden), and soon to be relocated outside of the garden. We lost our perfect relationship with God, and we introduced a veil to our existence. The perfect became flawed, and sin became lodged in our identity. It took root in our psychological being while infecting our DNA for future generations.

The human condition had become corrupted. Evidence of this corruption is easily identifiable on the news streams and in the quietness of our minds. Deep down, we know we are in need, and this impacts the way we think and the way we feel. We spend years and limited resources in attempting to mute this inner reality.

At Eden we:

- Wandered astray[6]
- Grew a dependency on, and an appetite for darkness[7]
- Broke the heart of God[8]
- Started the process of physically dying and spiritually dying[9]

At Eden, we became:

- Ignorant to the things of God[10]

4. Refer to 1 Cor 15:45 NIV
5. Refer to Rom 5:19; 1 Cor 15:22, 45 NIV
6. Refer to Isa 53:6 NIV
7. Refer to John 3:19 NIV
8. Refer to Hos 11: 1–8, John 11:35 NIV
9. Refer to 1 Pet 1:24; Eph 2:1 NIV
10. Refer to 1 Cor 2:14 NIV

- Spiritually blind[11]
- Enslaved to sin[12]
- Morally ruined[13]
- Hostile to God[14]

We became estranged to our true identity, and in doing so, our identity became jeopardized by our character. The reality of our closeness to God had become replaced with a deep longing for a closeness to God.

The reality was now becoming the desire.

We wanted to be known.

We wanted to be seen.

We replaced knowledge of God with self-limiting beliefs, and we built a society based on these self-limiting beliefs as our foundation.

The good news is of how Jesus looked at these deficiencies and loved us regardless. He chose to love us unconditionally, and he decided to implant his perfect being in our imperfect lives—the awesome choosing the flawed.

- In our hate he gave love
- When we were lost, he found us
- When we were broken, he fixed us
- When we were blind, he healed us
- When we were guilty, he justified us
- When we were enslaved, he paid our liberation price
- When we were ruined, he restored us
- When we were spiritually dead, he raised us to spiritual life

The flawed becoming flawesome.

As a species, we struggle to know who we are. Who we really are.

Try it. Ask a friend or group of people to tell who they are, avoiding questions allowing for basic answers such as providing their name, or stating what they do, or informing who they are married to, or basic information such as where they were born. Who are they? It will be revealing.

---

11. Refer to 2 Cor 4:4 NIV
12. Refer to John 8:34 NIV
13. Refer to Rom 7:18 NIV
14. Refer to Rom 8:7 NIV

Very few would offer an answer similar to "I am deeply loved, and I am greatly valued. I am an eternal being. I am physical and spiritual. I am worthy, and I am cherished."

Yet, this answer is the closest we can provide to our true identity. Many of us would have muted the spiritual (eternal) and heightened the physical (temporal), and this does lead to an unbalanced experience through life. Ignoring the spiritual aspect of life and focusing only on the material will generate uneven growth and a stunted understanding of who we are.

To fully know ourselves, we need to know Jesus and Jesus's role in our lives. Our true identity is found in Jesus. To fully know Jesus, we need to recognize Jesus as Lord and surrender to the Lordship of Christ. We are created for a relationship with God, felt through the deep hunger within our soul for intimacy. Intimacy with God and intimacy with humans. It is in this relationship that we find the fulfillment of love, the fulfillment of purpose, and emotional and psychological wholeness. It is where we find completeness.

When we fail to know and understand our identity fully, we become prone to uncertainty and insecurity, where we can quickly transfer this uncertainty and insecurity to the detriment of our relationships. Worse yet, we battle an economy dominated in parts to the task of turning citizens into consumers and turning needs into wants, while persuading us to participate in the super-sizing of our assets and lifestyle. If this isn't tragic enough, our adversary, Satan, is cunning in the art of seduction, offering a future where we would be king. We would be significant, and our names are to be known. An illusion upon which our needs and desires are met. A dreadful deception. Bait. Infatuation without the grounds of reality.

The priority of Satan is to lead us back to slavery, to enslave our minds, and end our freedom. To de-humanize us.

22

I Am Who I Am

My deepest awareness of myself is that I am deeply loved by Jesus Christ and I have done nothing to earn it or deserve it.

Brennan Manning[1]

We don't merely identify with God. Our very identity comes from God.

Our true identity is in God, determined by our Father, revealed in the person Jesus, and empowered through the Holy Spirit.

There are relatively few references in the Bible, where God uses the first tense to state who he is. Arguably the most significant of these statements is the account in Exodus where God declares to Moses:

> "I am who I am. This is what you are to say to the Israelites: 'I am has sent me to you.'"[2]

This is a self-declaration by God as to being God.

By declaring "I Am Who I Am" God is revealing his true nature. It encapsulates all the omni-statements[3] that we use to define our understanding of the nature and attributes of God. By declaring "I Am Who I Am," God speaks of his total self-sufficiency and the completeness of his self-existence. God is eternally constant. He is eternally unchanging and needs no help or

---

1. Manning, *The Ragamuffin Gospel*
2. Exod 3:14 NIV
3. Omnipotence, omniscience, omnificent, omnibenevolence, and omnipresence

assistance. His nature is not contingent on limiting factors nor impeded by external circumstances.

The context of this declaration was a conversation between Moses and God, a message that God would have Moses relay to Israel. Israel, a nation of slaves, preparing for liberation. It would be necessary for Israel to know the full nature of their liberator. God, as their liberator, would be Israel's constant hope. He was promising to liberate them, and they could be assured in his credentials as the eternal constant one with the power to fulfill their liberation.

Earlier, Pharaoh had been blinded to this reality and mocked Moses, he taunted Israel, and he mocked their God:

> Who is the LORD, that I should obey him and let Israel go? I do not know the LORD and I will not let Israel go.[4]

Pharaoh was immensely influential and powerful, a leader ruling over a great kingdom and refused to acknowledge a power greater than himself. He perceived the presence of God as a threat to his status. Pharaoh's response could be summarised as "I am Pharaoh. I am who I am. I will not submit to another."

Humanity has followed in this example set by Pharaoh and repeated by King Herod at the news of the birth of Jesus.

I am who I am. I will not submit to another. We can mistakenly become our point of reference and choose to be our version of I Am. By doing so, we deny our weakness and refuse our liberator. We then make plans within our limitations, and the scarce resources available through a more widespread societal deficiency. This self-proclaimed title of "I Am me" will inevitably become impeded as we face situations that we are not equipped to handle within our limited ability to overcome; in areas such as pain, anxiety, and relational breakdown. While on a macro-level, war. Wars have ravaged and blighted our existence. Wars start between nations, and fights begin between rivals as individualized "I Am Me" priorities clash.

Despite it being enough for God to state, "I am Who I am," it was not enough for humanity to accept. To help with our understanding of "I am Who I am," Jesus came to visibly demonstrate God through serving humanity and showing how this title is his.[5] Jesus revealed God and showed us how to respond to God.

God became known and revealed through the life of Jesus, and Jesus validated God through his character and his teaching. In the Gospel of John,

---

4. Exod 5:2 NIV
5. Refer to Col 1:15–20 NIV

we learn of seven *I Am* statements of Jesus. Statements expounding upon the fullness of God and the revealing of Jesus's identity, combined with the ability to understand how our identity is woven into who Jesus is.

Jesus the Bread of Life:

> I am the bread of life. Whoever comes to me will never go hungry, and whoever believes in me will never be thirsty.[6]

Humans have an inherited hunger and thirst for God, we are born with this spiritual need, and we will spend our lives searching to bring satisfaction to this need. We desire God.

Jesus affirms he is the one who will meet our spiritual hunger and our spiritual thirst, and in doing so, our identity is made complete.

Jesus the Light of the World:

> I am the light of the world. Whoever follows me will never walk in darkness, but will have the light of life.[7]

The light of Jesus will guide us out of every conceivable darkness we face. The darkness of loneliness, the night of regret, the darkness of fear. Jesus is affirming that he is our light, and once the light of Jesus illuminates every aspect of our lives, we discover the fullness of our identity.

Jesus the Gate:

> I am the gate; whoever enters through me will be saved. They will come in and go out, and find pasture.[8]

Jesus affirms that he is the only one who can lead us to God and lead us to heaven for eternity. The only way to attain eternal life is to enter through the gate of Jesus.

Jesus the Good Shepherd:

> I am the good shepherd. The good shepherd lays down his life for the sheep.[9]

Jesus is inherently good towards his sheep, and upon entering the earth, he demonstrated the benevolence of God. The second part of this affirmation reveals the tragedy and triumph of his death, a promise to the generations that he willingly laid down his life for us.

Jesus the Resurrection and the Life:

---

6. John 6:35 NIV
7. John 8:12 NIV
8. John 10:9 NIV
9. John 10:11 NIV

> I am the resurrection and the life. The one who believes in me will live, even though they die; and whoever lives by believing in me will never die.[10]

Jesus not only gives life, but he is life. No power, not even death, can take the life of one who is in Jesus. Our physical bodies will decay and die, but our lives will continue for eternity through Jesus, who is life. Through the Cross, Jesus secured victory over death, and death no longer has a hold on our lives.

Jesus the Way and the Truth and the Life:

> I am the way and the truth and the life. No one comes to the Father except through me.[11]

The crux of the matter, the heart of why Jesus came. The reason for his purpose on earth. He came to show us the way, he came to show us the truth, and he came to give life.

Jesus the Vine:

> I am the vine; you are the branches. If you remain in me and I in you, you will bear much fruit; apart from me you can do nothing.[12]

John's affirmation encapsulates the foundational principle of this book; we are perfected through Jesus, and this perfection comes through our belonging to Jesus. In this allegory, Jesus shows himself as the vine and describes us as the branches. As the vine, he is our source, and he is our sustenance. When connected to Jesus, our identity can be liberated and fully realized, and we become effective in bearing fruit on behalf of the kingdom of Heaven.

Jesus meets our every identity need.

I work within the leadership of a small boutique charity, and each year we potentially impact more people than Jesus did during his life. Over the past decade, I'm convinced we've affected more people than Jesus did. We're only a small charity. Collectively, as the citizens of the kingdom of Heaven, we are doing great things and the statistics of what we achieve is phenomenal. A study conducted a few years back saw attempts made at monetizing the effect of the church on a particular nation, and the result was staggering. The impact was grossly underestimated and mostly unreported. The social and economic benefits of the kingdom of God, in a host nation, carry vast

---

10. John 11:25–26 NIV
11. John 14:6 NIV
12. John 15:5 NIV

significance; social cohesion, welfare programs, a beacon of light during times of national tragedy, a place of celebration, a place where family memories are etched. The pulling together of followers of Jesus to meet societal needs is like no other. It is the goodness of the good news.

We're empowered through the Holy Spirit to continue the work of Jesus,[13] and the quality of our response to this challenge is mostly dependent on the confidence we have in our identity. Jesus said, "heal the sick." However, should we consider the sickness being from God for humility, or the illness being a consequence of sin, or through a lack of faith, then we will struggle to pray for the sick confidently. We pray for the sick because Jesus told us to, we only complicate this by our doubt. The same principle exists for speaking the good news. Should we doubt the good news message, we may struggle to appear authentic. When we misrepresent the Gospel message by only highlighting the happiness of the Gospel, we do an injustice. The Lausanne Covenant of 1974 carries the following statement:

> In issuing the gospel invitation we have no liberty to conceal the cost of discipleship.[14]

There is a high cost involved in following Jesus. In many of our cultures, we have segments of society prone to the entitlement philosophy of life. It can, therefore, remain a challenge for the cost of discipleship considered a good thing when placed on the framework of entitlement.

Unless we are securely grafted to the vine of Jesus, our identity and the understanding of our identity will remain deficient. We can see this in the physical. There is an almost natural desire to know how we are connected. For the adopted, there comes a time where many will desire to know their birth parents. In the country that's embraced my family, many people want to discover their European roots, and upon discovery, speak of a deeper level of completeness. Spiritually, it's the same. We possess the spiritual desire to know our spiritual lineage. We all do seek this. Some are actively seeking. Others are sensing a craving without the insight to put words or actions around this desire.

We remain incomplete until we are grafted into the vine of Jesus. Deficient in our sense of belonging and incomplete in fully knowing our identity. When grafted to Jesus, the works of Jesus become natural. The branch has no power of its own to produce fruit and has no ability of its own to sustain life. The branch only has life-giving power and fruit-bearing capacity through being grafted into the vine. Unlike in the natural, we have

---

13. Refer to Acts 1:8, Rom 8:11, Rom 8:26, Rom 15:13, Eph 3:16–19 NIV
14. The Lausanne Covenant

freewill to disconnect from God and become independent from the branch that gives life.

For humanity, it remains a false-claim and is profoundly misguided to declare self-sufficiency. The hope for humanity is to be found only in our abandonment of self-sovereignty and autonomy and our confession of God's sovereignty in our mortal and flawed lives.

The importance of knowing our identity is of the utmost urgency.

23

The World Awaits your Identity

Once you label me you negate me.
SØREN KIERKEGAARD[1]

I HAVE CONFIDENCE IN knowing who I am. There is no conflict or deficiency in my identity. God loves me, and this is my identity. It answers every philosophical question that can hinder me. Who am I? How did I get here? Where am I going? What's my purpose? Why is there suffering? Those defining questions, coupled with the need to know I have lived and have toiled for a purpose. That I have left something worthy to pass on to future generations, people do want to matter. I want to matter.

I am seen, and I am known. This is my identity.

My character, on the other hand, has deficiencies and lack, and at times, significant lack. I enter a Board room, and I feel insignificant. I am asked a question to which I am well versed, and I spend the night rehearsing how I wish I had answered. I feel awkward in a room of peers and pretend to be engaged in a significant task on my phone simply through inferiority and momentarily forgetting how to connect with fellow humans. I start to succeed, and Imposter Syndrome kicks in. I consider my writing and wish I had the understanding of Tolstoy, the philosophy of Hugo, the vulnerability of Yancey, the curiosity of Bryson, the imagination of Lewis, the vision of Milton, and the insight of Orwell, and conclude that I have no place in the

---

1. Quote attributed to Kierkegaard

written world. I launched my first book without the confidence to promote it. I reflect on the years of focusing on my weaknesses and how to overcome them, and how even this exercise adds to my list of things unfinished, and this focus on my shortcomings itself becomes overwhelming and turns out to be my latest weakness. I receive congratulations, and in a well-used proclamation of false-humility, I say, "it was nothing, really." The times Sarah and I are sulking with each other, and we both forget the reason why.

I wish I prayed more, gave more, invested more in the next generation. At times I still look in the mirror and see the pain and hurt behind the reflection. I remain in the process of my mind being renewed and transformed to reflect my inherited true nature as being perfected through Jesus. I continue as a work in progress.

My experience of being perfected through Christ will not be fully realized on this battle-scarred earth, where even the perfection of God's love is muted to differing degrees through the pain and perils of my life.

Yet my desire for the discovery of and the revealing of my true identity, manifesting itself in the wisdom of the Holy Spirit, will help to advance the cause of humanity beyond compare, where I join a growing global community of followers of Jesus living out authentic and purposeful identities. This bridges heaven and earth and brings healing to the nations and peace to the suburbs.

People can spend a lifetime without truly knowing who they are; or living up to family or societal expectations of who they ought to be. We can all too easily experience a life of regret and the fear of failing to live up to self-determined and self-imposed expectations.

You are the crown of God's creation. You are more than existence and more than useful, as beautifully highlighted below:

> The crown of God's creation is a new creature, a creature that can sound the heartbeat of its Creator. That creature, made male and female, reflects God's relational richness. The human family is to join God in the ongoing work of creation.[2]

Identity is who we are, rather than what we are. Identity is confidence in the person Jesus rather than position, qualification, family, status, or social networks. Elevating these areas above Jesus will jeopardize the quality of life. Yet, by raising Jesus to the highest place in our lives motivates us to develop family relationships and societal networks to an even higher degree than we could ever possibly achieve without having Jesus as Lord of our lives.

---

2. The Voice Bible, *Commentary of Genesis*

Earlier, I wrote about the first known questions to humanity. One from the serpent and the other from God, reaching to the core of humanity. "Did God say." "Where are you." The first question sowed the seed of doubt; "Did God say." A seed now lodged deep within our human condition and has since grown to a formidable tree with extensive and deep roots.

Many people now doubt the reliability of these two questions. In 1928, William Isaac Thomas developed the Thomas theorem or the Thomas dictum based on the assumption:

> If men define situations as real, they are real in their consequences.[3]

This theorem was later termed a "self-fulfilling prophecy" by American sociologist Robert K Merton.[4] In the case of doubt, a self-fulfilling prophecy is realized. Eve doubted, and we now doubt this first instance of doubt. Or, we at least challenge the historical context of the first recorded expression of doubt. Here, Satan achieved an extraordinary accomplishment. He integrated doubt with our identity, providing him ongoing and open access to our minds—such a subtle but devastating achievement. In many ways, Satan attacks in just one area of our lives: our identity, and he succeeds in this pursuit by turning the key of doubt that we've inherited.

To discover true identity requires an understanding of the human constitution. Earlier, we considered how people struggle to give a reasonable answer to the question: "Who are you," and we hypothesized that many would give descriptive or informative answers only and failing to provide confidence in who they really are. We looked at scripture, providing answers such as "you are loved," "you are created," and "you are important."

As revolutionary as these answers are, we require a mechanism to believe these declarations; less they fall into the category of fairy-tale, nonsense, or being believable but just not to the extent they reach my struggles and the need to bring holistic wellness to my life. We need a receptor and a decoder. We need a basic understanding of the human constitution.

How are we made?

---

3. Thomas, *Oxford Reference*
4. Refer to https://en.wikipedia.org/wiki/Self-fulfilling_prophecy

24

To Be a Human?

The line separating good and evil passes not through states, nor between classes, nor between political parties either—but right through every human heart—and through all human hearts. This line shifts. Inside us, it oscillates with the years. And even within hearts overwhelmed by evil, one small bridgehead of good is retained.

ALEKSANDR I. SOLZHENITSYN[1]

THE SEARCH FOR IDENTITY void of God will never bring completeness and will result in an ongoing elusive search for self, leading to more questions than answers.

It's interesting how hard it can be for many people to answer this question. How are we made? What is the structure of the human being?

Are we a whole, a unitary whole? Holistic beings? Are we made up of one, two, or three parts? Are we fragmented and easily segmented into components? If so, what are these components? How do they impact our identity? How does our understanding of the human constitution change our contribution to society?

Understanding our identity requires knowing who we are and knowing what we are while knowing the source of perfected identity.

---

1. Mahoney, *Aleksandr Solzhenitsyn*

People belong to God. God knows this. Unfortunately, many humans fail to recognize this. Our identity is perfected in God, and from our identity, we experience validation. And it is through God's validation we gain purpose and imitate God through our conduct and behavior while discovering our identity in its fullness.

The ability to discover the fullness of our identity requires us to identify with the one whose image we bear.[2] Through acknowledging dependence on our creator, we become sons and daughters of God and forever will be citizens of a never-ending, flawless, and perfect home. Everlasting pure love. Eternal, pain-free living.[3] Infinite beauty.

All that is required is simple surrender. Surrendering our flawed lives in exchange for liberation, and receiving temporary flawesome lives with the promise of eternal flawless living. To live well within the human body.

---

2. Refer to Gen 1:27, 1 Cor 15:49 NIV
3. Refer to Isa 2:3–4, Isa 11:6–9, Rev 21:4 NIV

25

Living Inside a Human Body

I believe in Liberty for all men: the space to stretch their arms and their souls, the right to breathe and the right to vote, the freedom to choose their friends, enjoy the sunshine, and ride on the railroads, uncursed by color; thinking, dreaming, working as they will in a kingdom of beauty and love.

WILLIAM EDWARD BURGHARDT DU BOIS[1]

THE MOST CHALLENGING QUESTION is the simplest. Do we know how to live inside of our bodies?

It has become a point of personal interest as to how we've achieved many triumphs as a human race, yet we can remain uncertain about what makes us human and how to reside inside of our body. It is easier to say we live in this country or that country, as to say we live inside a body that comprises the spiritual and the natural. It's bewildering how we have put humans on the Moon, sent robots to Mars, and built a worldwide web without knowing the spiritual components of what makes us human.

To enjoy the fullness of being human, we need to consider the spiritual (the immaterial aspect of life, intangible, and eternal) and the physical (the material aspect of life; physical, tangible, and temporal) and to know how they relate. Several years back I was struck with a profound awareness: do I

---

1. Du Bois, National Public Radio

know who I am, closely followed by the realization of possessing a spirit and a soul but without the words to describe their unique and differentiating qualities.

Dichotomism and trichotomism are two theories to help guide our understanding of the human constitution; theories providing a framework of scriptural knowledge, proposing how we are both spiritual in nature and human in nature.

Whereas the dichotomist view proposes a two-way division made up of the soul and the body, the trichotomist view would offer a three-way division compromising spirit, soul, and body. Within the dichotomist view, however, spirit and soul can be regarded as interchangeable terms referring to the same spiritual reality. Within the trichotomist view, spirit and soul are distinguishable and carry different functions with the soul having an earthward trajectory and the spirit having a heavenward trajectory. Both views would consider the body as representing the flesh.

The trichotomist view versus the dichotomist view is not necessarily contradictory; instead, they can be considered complementary. Both speak of the spiritual aspect of human life and the physical aspect of human life, and the importance of both elements. They remain qualified theories supported by scripture. Their points of agreement exceed any differences, and the importance of conclusively deciding between the two-part versus the three-part theory may not be necessary. The trichotomist approach remains simpler to explain as the dichotomist theory leaves room for debating the soul and spirit.

The challenge remains not to take each theory to an extreme through over-emphasizing the mystical or down-playing God's absolute interest in the physical, the intellectual, and the emotional condition. Neither extreme is healthy. Both theories do complement each other in the importance of recognizing the complex nature of humans. Whether three-part or two-part, we are created with the ability to enter a loving relationship with God, who we can call Abba[2] or papa.

By making the differentiation between our various elements too fragmented, we run the risk of viewing life as being inherently compartmentalized. In a categorized version of life, Satan may possess the soul, and the Holy Spirit inhabits the spirit. A type of internal spiritual tug-of-war plays out where both entities are appealing to our flesh to act in one way or to act in another—God's home versus Satan's residence. For the non-follower of Jesus, it is a horrific reality where a soul can be possessed. For the follower of Jesus, it is perhaps more a case of coming under oppression, where seeds of

---

2. Refer to Rom 8:15 NIV

doubt are sown into our imperfect minds. This is how we can exhibit values of the fallen kingdom expressed through our character while having the security of belonging to God.

Be us a division of two, or be us a division of three, should leave us with a sense of awe and wonder rather than confusion and argument. We are wonderfully made[3] and deeply loved by God, who willingly resides in our lives to bring transformation from the inside out.

During our stay on earth, we do have an enemy intent on our destruction. The Apostle Paul informs this not as a physical struggle, instead, a spiritual struggle.[4] The devil would perhaps enjoy no higher activity than to ruin our ability to feel loved and to extend love. The role of doubt, unfortunately, does leave us as easy prey.

We are more than sensual. We are more than an animal. We have a spiritual constitution, made in the spiritual image of God while reflecting the natural image of our earthly parents. God truly is our Father, and he called our family tree "very good."[5] The flawed and damaged aspect of our DNA is not an inheritance from a loving God, and he will redeem this damage and unconditionally love us through our fractures. To the point whereby he carried the pain of these scars to the cross, and we look forward to the day our bodies are renewed through resurrection.

His perfect glory. His perfect purposes fulfilled through our imperfect and flawed constitution.

Humans are both physical and spiritual.

---

3. Refer to Ps 139:14 NIV
4. Refer to 2 Cor 10:4–5 NIV
5. Refer to Gen 1:31 NIV

26

What Makes us Human?

Human brains aren't built for self-rule.
Professor Shawn Rosenberg[1]

WHAT MAKES US HUMAN is that which separates us from animals.

I have very little desire and no particular reason, within the pages of this book, to promote one view over the other. The dichotomist view verses the trichotomist view. I do hope to agree with both theories and move forward with the tested and the agreed-upon position that we are both spiritual and physical, and this impacts our everyday lives.

The Physical

The body is the physical part of our being, similar to general life on earth. We possess a body just as a dog, a bird, and other forms of life. Even, to some degree, plant life. Our human body primarily interacts with the material world through the senses (sight, smell, hearing, taste, and touch); it remains temporal and will one day decompose, where the dust returns to the earth.[2]

---

1. Rick Shenkman, 8th September 2019 reporting on a speech delivered by Professor Shawn Rosenberg at the 2019 International Society of Political Psychologists annual meeting, Lisbon, Portugal
2. Refer to Eccl 3:20, Job 10:9 NIV

The human body is more advanced and sophisticated than that of a plant, or that of lesser sentient animals, and this is where our nature becomes spiritual.

The Spiritual

What now provides complete separation and uniqueness to the human is our eternal and spiritual nature. It is the spirit that sets us apart from the animal kingdom, and it is the spiritual where we are created for transformation through the renewing of the mind. God highly values us to such a degree that he identifies us as "the temple of the Holy Spirit."[3]

While some animals may be considered as sentient beings with the ability to feel and possess some level of awareness of how life happens around them, they function in a much less complicated manner to that of humans. Elephants are considered as exhibiting self-awareness, and dolphins are observed as being creative. Other life-forms, besides a physical frame, have no commonality with humans and simply exist. They reproduce and provide sustenance for life. Humans, on the other hand, are deeply intricate with a great depth of interconnectedness and a great yearning to belong.

We are also psychological beings with unique personalities, complex emotions, and with the means to reason. We engage with life at high levels of awareness, and we can be affectionate, can imagine, have the mechanism to retain memory, and the essential quality to act upon our conscience. We respond to dynamic situations through feelings and passions, desires, and appetites. We can love, and we can hate, create peace, and start a war. We can lust, and we can pursue innocence. We can choose to accept others, and we can decide to reject others. We are logical, aware, and emotional.

Our spiritual nature drives us to form meaningful relationships, and it is our spiritual nature that compels us towards the community. It is our spiritual nature that allows us to respond to the spiritual and to fathom the depths of God. The point of connection between humans and God.

Whereas love would generate from the spirit, lust would generate from the sensual nature of humans. For this reason, practices such as hedonism and narcissism are detrimental to the human experience and harmful to our communities. Any hedonistic or narcissistic pursuit of individualized pleasure and self-centric obsession will impact those closest. These pursuits will have additional negative impacts on those who are perceived as being the objects of ultimate desire, and for those perceived as being roadblocks to this desire of self-indulgence and pleasure.

The hollowness of hedonism and narcissism is of how the unobtainable destination is merely an illusion, and the pursuit of this illusion will be

---

3. 1 Cor 6:19 NIV

marked by frustration and great depths of sadness. It is a great tragedy of life where one cannot find fulfillment within their current situation.

It's perhaps a point of irony that the hedonist seeks ultimate pleasure through self-centric living, yet, it is the follower of Jesus who finds complete joy through Jesus-centric living, a joy almost describable as hedonistic: the perfect fulfillment of desire. Ultimate pleasure comes from God, not to be pursued in its own right, rather, within the divine order of God's loving-kindness towards us. There is an irrefutable spiritual dynamic at work that would see how making Jesus Lord of our lives, results in the ability to live life in its fullest measure.

We may not be hedonistic or narcissistic, yet there are many self-centric activities we become involved with. Even the best of us can succumb to self-centric choices, yet we do not need to be defined by this lifestyle.

We are spiritual beings as much as we are physical beings; this is what makes humans unique amongst all other life forms.

And it is this unique quality of being spiritual that raises questions reaching the very nature of what it means to be a human.

If God cares for us, cares for us as a whole, we must care for what God cares for. We must look after our physical bodies, as we must look after our minds and to look after our emotions. If we're to be active on this earth, we need to maintain the physical transport we live within. We do not have the liberty to neglect our physical frame. Yet, there is often a fine line between maintaining physical health and the idolization of the body, where we can become addicted to the wrong food or addicted to exercise, these are both extremes that we need to guard against.

In John, Jesus makes a declaration of intent; "I have come that they may have life and have it to the full."[4] This declaration becomes a manifesto for the ultimate betterment of the human condition. Jesus uses the term "life" representing the entirety of the human constitution: spiritual, physical, and psychological. To be recipients of Jesus's life-to-the-full promise is to be discovered through a relationship with Jesus.

Jesus made a further, and a far-reaching declaration by summarising the law of the Old Testament with two simple commands:

- Love God: Love the Lord your God with all your heart and with all your soul and with all your mind and with all your strength[5]
- Love others: Love your neighbor as yourself[6]

---

4. John 10:10 NIV
5. Refer to Mark 12:30 NIV
6. Refer to Mark 12:31 NIV

A relationship where the first recipient, being God, and second recipients, being others, are so knitted together, it perhaps seems unnecessary to try and bring a hierarchy between the two.

To love our neighbor as ourselves requires us to love ourselves, and to love ourselves requires that we know ourselves. Jesus speaks of four areas where we can voluntarily love God: we can love God through our heart, through our soul, through our mind, and we can love God through our strength.[7] We do not want to love our neighbor through a self-imposed deficiency in any of these four areas. Alternatively, we need to stay away from adopting and promoting ourselves through a sense of an over-idealized persona.

Modern trends are seeing the attempt to mould our real lives based around a fake persona generated through social media. Although in relative infancy, this phenomenon of commoditizing our persona through social-platforms is gaining momentum. We can now market our identity as would a marketeer develop brand awareness around a product. The individual, or at least the online representation of the individual, becomes a marketable commodity through personal brand awareness. Often, this branded identity becomes monetized. We exaggerate the positives of our lives, or at times, magnify the negatives in our lives, to a watching world. Much of this watching world suffers a deficit in genuine validation, and they experience confusion when identifying their sense of value and purpose. They need to know they are known. They are seen, rather than just looked at. When this need for validation interacts with exaggerated social personas, we see the likely scenario of the condition known as FOMO (the Fear of Missing Out), as well as heightened comparison and the subsequent social ills that follow.

It becomes easy for the social viewer to seek validation through a constant source of fake, exaggerated, and misleading messaging based on a profoundly complex system of algorithms that lacks ethics and a basis of qualified support or authentic peer review.

Reaching the complete fullness of life will rarely, if ever, be experienced this side of heaven. We are journeying towards perfection. A side-effect of this reality, however, is how we will love people through our deficiency, and it is through this personal deficiency that people will experience pain and hurt. Yet, our weakness is more than compensated through God's perfect love in our lives:

> But he said to me, "My grace is sufficient for you, for my power is made perfect in weakness." Therefore, I will boast all the more gladly about my weaknesses, so that Christ's power may rest on

---

7. Refer to Mark 12:30 NIV

me. That is why, for Christ's sake, I delight in weaknesses, in insults, in hardships, in persecutions, in difficulties. For when I am weak, then I am strong.[8]

For this reason, it remains of great importance that society, united as one, does journey in the love of God. A journey that reaches our neighbors, near, and far.

Our love for our neighbor needs to reach the full person. Not just to that which we consider spiritual. We need to demonstrate a love that reaches all of humanity; social needs, psychological needs, physical needs, emotional needs, economic needs, and of course, spiritual needs. But we should not presume we can solve personal problems through a simple spiritual response. We need health in all areas of life, and this will include:

- The disciplines of prayer, study, and fellowship
- The practical disciplines of diet, exercise, and avoiding toxic or damaging relationships
- A commitment to the vulnerable in our community. Those groups identified by God as being prone to vulnerability, for those who are experiencing powerlessness and other forms of distress

God's deliberate advocacy of these groups requires that we, too, become their advocates, speaking on their behalf.[9] The vulnerable groups identified through the Bible are the widow, the orphan, the foreigner (the marginalized, the disadvantaged, the vulnerable). The listing in the twenty-first century may be different and will vary between societies and systems of government, but the principle remains. Advocate on behalf of the vulnerable.

Today, the widow, the orphan, and the foreigner represent any person or grouping of people who are vulnerable and in need of protection from governments and societies who mistreat them and who dis-empower them. The security of the vulnerable is of the highest importance to God. The emotionally vulnerable. The economically vulnerable. The physically vulnerable. The spiritually vulnerable. The vulnerable need to be safe, respected, and given a voice to express their views and opinions. In today's world, the widow and the orphan will be the refugee and the slave. The child soldier and the trafficked. Those with differing opinions that relegate them to vulnerability. Those whose ideologies and lifestyles differ from our own, but through their ideologies and lifestyle, become vulnerable. Those who face disadvantages through other persons' poor and unethical use of

---

8. 2 Cor 12:9–10 NIV
9. Refer to Exod 22:21–22, Deut 10:17–19, Jer 22:3–4, Jas 1:27 NIV

positional power, be it a national leader, spouse, or boss. This is why the need for churches and organizations reaching these groups is of vital importance to the advancement of the Kingdom of Heaven on earth.

God validates all people, and our response to this needs to happen.

Attempts to separate the physical from the spiritual when meeting a person's needs will be limited in its effectiveness. God cares for the whole person, and the good news that we are to share needs to be good news to the entire person; otherwise, we limit God and diminish God's transformational plan for personal wholeness. In focusing only on the narrowest of good news messages, we construct barriers and create distance. God is interested in the whole, and continually ministers to and transforms the whole, through partnering with each of us.

With a rudimentary understanding that humans are both physical and spiritual, we move forward to the reality and question of how we navigate the conflict between choosing righteousness and denying temptation in our daily walk with Jesus.

The Human Being. A creature created for relationship with God. Higher than the animal kingdom. Higher than the angelic nation. In Eden, we enjoyed this relationship through the full array of our senses, the full spectrum of emotions, and through an undivided heart. This perfect communion was broken and will be restored in the future. We now live in the gap between perfection, and we build community and relationship in this breach, the gap between Eden and Heaven. Although we wait for full restoration, glimpses of perfection remain a reality.

27

Created for Community

*Loneliness and the feeling of being uncared for
and unwanted are the greatest poverty.*

MOTHER TERESA[1]

THE MOST BASIC OF human desire is the desire to be loved. Yet it remains an easy task to jeopardize our ability to be loved through doubt (to doubt we are worthy of love); through fear (to erect barriers of self-defense to protect from the fear of failure); or through inadequacy (telling ourselves we are unworthy of love). We need to take a role in assuring doubt, fear, and inadequacy have no power to rob us of our experience of love. We are created for love.

It's perhaps of little wonder how the battle many of us face is in our relationship to love. Loneliness. Isolation. Low self-worth. Toxic behavior. These are all symptoms of a love-deficit. One of our biggest challenges is to let ourselves be loved. To love and to be loved.

The origin of our story is simple; God loves us, and God was pleased to create us. God went through the same life-changing amazement and sense of awe experienced by any new parent at the birth of their child. We are co-created; our human parents are giving our genetic make-up and our physical attributes, while God gives spirit. Our physical bodies will reflect our parents while our spirit will reflect God. We receive our spiritual inheritance

---

1. Teresa, as quoted on Goodreads

from God while inheriting a flawed body with defects and physical problems that have taken root in our natural genealogy for thousands of years.[2]

God's love is free, yet, the experience and benefit of this love require practice. When we do not engage with God's love, we experience separation and spiritual loneliness.

Loneliness is a significant problem facing humanity today. Be it the loneliness stemming from social disconnectedness or the isolation arising from the lack of a genuine and authentic depth of social engagement. I made the statement earlier of how the need to be known and the need to be seen are of great significance. We need to be known. We need to be seen. Experiencing deficiency in either or both of these areas will magnify this feeling of loneliness.

Returning to the conversation at the start of this book where, through my self-diagnosed perception of insignificance, I had reached the unfounded conclusion that I am "not seen." For Tin, his self-diagnosed perception of insecurity led him to the self-generated and invalid claim of "not being known."

In both instances, we concentrated on misconstrued versions of our identity rather than focusing on our perfected identity grounded firmly in God's validation of our lives.

God's validation results in our lives being valid. True for Tin, right for me, and accurate for each of us.

We will all, at one time or another, experience a range of similar feelings of inadequacy and insignificance, and these feelings become real as we experience them. We do not doubt them, and we do not pretend they are not there. This is why Jesus died, and this is why the Holy Spirit came. Jesus died to perfect us, and the Holy Spirit continues this perfecting work.

We are an immense combination of the natural and the spiritual, and we are as complex as we are unique. God refers to this as being "fearfully and wonderfully made."[3] As the Holy Spirit highlights areas in our life that remain incompatible with perfection, we can be encouraged to take these as insight from our personal guide and respond to them, overcome them, and be freed from them. Let God do what he does best: liberation.

A guiding hypothesis of this book, similar to the need to be known and seen, is the need for genuine and authentic love. As humans, we are designed to give and receive significance, to give and receive care, and to give and receive love. When we do not fulfill this need, we experience emotions and reactions that are to the detriment of successful living.

---

2. Principles discussed in Matthews *The Nine Veils*
3. Ps 139:14 NIV

Desmond Tutu writes:

> The solitary human being is a contradiction in terms.[4]

He continues:

> We are made for complementarity. We are created for a delicate network of relationships, of interdependence with our fellow human beings. . . We belong in one family—God's family, the human family. . . the greatest good is communal harmony.[5]

Tutu's quote stands in stark contrast to the position taken by former British Prime Minister Margaret Thatcher, who, in 1987, in making a statement advocating individualism, infamously spoke, "there's no such thing as society."[6] Decades later, during the COVID-19 pandemic, Prime Minister Boris Johnson, well aware of Thatcher's controversial quote, declared a contradiction to his predecessor by announcing "there really is such a thing as society."[7]

Politicians, social engineers, economists, and philosophers can spend eternity debating the role, limits, and function of society, while the mother holding their newborn for the first time answers this within her heart. God knew from the start. He knew it is not good for us to be alone.[8]

Community is the heart of society, and within the community, there needs to be safety from all that would harm. And not just protection, but the ability to fully develop as humans and to be productive.

God does not intend for us to be lonely and isolated. Loneliness has been described as a "homesickness for God."[9] Indeed, God created us for the community, and God is calling us into a relationship with him and a relationship with other humans. Perhaps why isolation through solitary confinement within the penal system is a dreaded consequence.

There is a fine line between self-development for the sake of personal gain, and self-development for the community. Our lives need to be turned to God and postured towards the community. As parents, we observed with great interest and adoration the development of our children, their first smile, crawl, their first step, and first word.

We marveled at their development.

4. Tutu, *God is Not a Christian*
5. Tutu, *God is Not a Christian*
6. Women's Own "Interview with Margaret Thatcher"
7. Johnson, "There is such a thing as society"
8. Refer to Gen 2:18 NIV
9. Quote appears in Gumbel, *Bible in One Year*

We had created a person growing daily with self-sufficiency that would one day see them leave our family home and venture beyond the garden gate. With a deep sense of wonder, we would observe each developmental stage with the hope that the love, culture, traditions, quirks, values, and shared family history would create a lifetime of freewill relationship firmly rooted in the values and the priorities of our family.

Such reveals a spiritual mystery. Our children leave home and create distance to establish their place in the world, a movement from complete parental dependency to maturity and independence. The parental relationship does not end, nor should it lose value and importance. It changes—changes in the sense of function, authority, and reliance. I've found a new appreciation for this parental relationship, and although it has changed in geography, it has deepened at the same time.

Our relationship with God, however, works differently. God advocates for an increasingly closer and increasingly more significant intimate relationship with us, a daily deepening of communication and connection. In the physical, we become less cleaved. In the spiritual, we are to become increasingly cleaved. In the physical, our self-development would tend to create physical distance with our earthly parents. In the spiritual, our development leads to a closing of this gap.

This level of intimacy requested by God is not to create an unhealthy-dependence or a controlling influence. This intimacy is for our benefit. Whereas human intimacy is very limited in its inclusiveness, intimacy with God is not exclusive in the sense that God would have us find full security and confidence in our identity to be able to reach out to others with this same hope of love. We call this the Great Commission, and to fulfill this Great Commission will require self-development. A self-development for the sake of others and not for personal gain. Whereas self-reliance ruins intimacy, self-development increases intimacy.

Losing sight of a child, even momentarily, has a profound impact on the parent. There is an immediate and severe sense of concern, and the longer the child remains missing, the tighter this grip of concern becomes. A parent will attest to this grip being all-consuming. Concern leading to worry, anxiety, and then guilt sweeping over the parent. Regardless of whether this is misplaced guilt or not, guilt has no care for origin; it just impacts. The parent's life, their purpose for existence, become focused on the need to find their child.

As a child, I put my parents through this experience on many occasions. At the beach, in the sea, on a mountain, in the theatre, and the city. My parents can confirm this, to the point in which they became embarrassed to call the police yet again. In Luke chapter two, we meet the parents of Jesus (Mary and Joseph) returning home from Jerusalem after the Festival of Passover. Unbeknownst to Mary and Joseph, Jesus had stayed behind to spend time sitting with the teachers in the temple courts. Jesus listened to the teachers and asked them questions. Luke records how the teachers were "amazed at his understanding and his answers."[10] In hindsight, their amazement could perhaps have paused for enough time to ask a simple question, "where are your parents?" The Bible records how Jesus was found in the temple after three days.[11] Mary said, "Son, why have you treated us like this? Your father and I have been anxiously searching for you."[12] Jesus answered, "Why were you searching for me. . .Didn't you know I had to be in my Father's house."[13] Luke records how Mary and Joseph did not understand Jesus's answer. Nonetheless, Jesus left the temple to go home with his parents. Luke provides the following observation "[Jesus] went down to Nazareth with them and was obedient to them."[14]

I often wonder if these days saw Jesus growing into the fullness of the knowledge of his identity; perhaps the discussions in the temple were an investigation of the prophets of old. Was he learning his purpose?

This story of boy Jesus at the temple ends with the summary, "And Jesus grew in wisdom and stature, and in favor with God and man."

Jesus was developing to become a teenager.

Preceding this account of Jesus in the temple as a 12-year old, Luke recounts an earlier time Jesus was taken to the temple in Jerusalem to be presented to the Lord. Sharing similarities of Jesus at the temple as a 12-year old, this story too ends with a statement regarding the development of Jesus, "And the child grew and became strong; he was filled with wisdom, and the grace of God was on him."[15]

Both stories of Jesus at the temple summarise the development of the man Jesus.

- Jesus grew in stature
- Jesus grew in wisdom
- Jesus became strong
- Jesus developed favor with man
- Jesus developed favor with God

10. Luke 2:47 NIV
11. Refer to Luke 2:41–52
12. Luke 2:48 NIV
13. Luke 2:49 NIV abridged
14. Luke 2:51 NIV
15. Luke 2:40 NIV

In the book of Hebrews, The Apostle Paul continues this theme of the development of Jesus:

- Jesus learned obedience[16]
- Jesus was made perfect[17]

Jesus's life was one of discovery and development.

Stating Jesus learned obedience and was made perfect can lead to the assumption that he was not always obedient, and he was not always perfect. A minefield of discussion. Was Jesus the perfect baby that no mother has ever had? Did Jesus cry when thirsty? How was Jesus as a two-year-old? Did he, through exploration and innocence, spill things, break things and seek attention at all hours of the night?

I consider these observations (learned obedience and being made perfect) speak of Jesus discovering his true identity. He became fully aware of himself, fully aware of God, and fully aware of others. He was finding the fullness of his identity.

Whereas we discover our perfection through salvation and discipleship, Jesus found his perfection from birth. Jesus knew of sin but had not sinned.[18] On the contrary, we do know sin, and we actively partake in sin. We needed one of our kind, Jesus, the second Adam[19] to redeem us as our kinsman-redeemer. To be an authentic kinsman-redeemer, the kinsman does need to be from the same family, the same kin, and to share the same bloodline. We see this in anthropological terms, and we see this in legal terms during family inheritance, where next-of-kin denotes the deceased's closest living relatives. Jesus truly is our everlasting father,[20] and we are indeed his children.

Jesus developed as does any human; growing and maturing in the four overlapping areas common to us all:

- mental development (wisdom)
- physical development (stature)
- social and emotional development (favor with people)
- spiritual development (favor with God)

Jesus grew in character, and he grew in his competency.

16. Refer to Heb 5:8 NIV
17. Refer to Heb 2:10, Heb 5:8–9, Heb 7:28 NIV
18. Refer to 2 Cor 5:21 NIV
19. Refer to 1 Cor 15:45–48 NIV
20. Refer to Isa 9:6 NIV

CREATED FOR COMMUNITY

Tradition would have Jesus as a carpenter, a trade requiring the development of skill and knowledge. As he grew, he mastered the simplest of motor-skill through to the advanced artisan skills needed as a tradesman. He grew in wisdom; he grew in knowledge and developed in understanding his identity and purpose.

Jesus developed.

Likewise, we need to develop. We have an identity to be fully discovered, and we have a purpose to be fully lived out. It's a tragedy that many do not recognize this.

Nature will have us develop those involuntary areas such as height and appearance while we need to pursue those voluntary areas of development such as knowledge, skill, strength, and character.

The Bible speaks of voluntary development:

- First Peter[21] tells us to crave pure spiritual milk to grow up.
- Hebrews[22] tells us to move beyond spiritual milk and partake in solid spiritual food to be trained with the discernment to distinguish good from evil.

And Paul the Apostle advocates development through the provision of spiritual gifts. Ten gifts mentioned, but we are challenged to desire the greater gifts eagerly.[23]

Likewise, Galatians 5 tells us to practice the fruit of the spirit. Whereas, Romans[24] and James[25] provides evidence, again, of the need for human development.

These voluntary areas for development will take persistence, and they need effort, as summarised in Romans.[26] Yet, they are necessary for the disciple to mature beyond the stage of being a spiritual-infant.

As Jesus developed, so must we.

Life on this flawed planet will, should we succumb, facilitate regression, and a general decline in the quality of life. We see this in the physical where sickness, poverty, and examples of poor governance have led to countless suffering to millions, and we can see this in the spiritual where James[27] gives insight as to a decline of the human state.

21. Refer to 1 Pet 2:2 NIV
22. Refer to Heb 5:12–14 NIV
23. Refer to 1 Cor 12, 13 NIV
24. Refer to Rom 5:3–5 NIV
25. Refer to Jas 1:4 NIV
26. Refer to Rom 5:3–4 NIV
27. Refer to Jas 1:14–16 NIV

Some humans are unfortunate as to the time and place of their birth. The Jew born in Poland in the 1930s. The child born in Hiroshima in the early 1940s. The enslaved of West Africa between the sixteenth centuries and nineteenth centuries; the thousands dying daily through COVD-19; the children caught amid the current Syrian Civil War where the consequences of the decisions of others have resulted in untold suffering for the individual.

Suffering does have an origin, and it does have a cure.

We are currently in a global pandemic with borders and societies closing down as the numbers of infected reach the millions. Of importance to fighting COVID-19 is identifying Patient Zero; to trace the roots of the virus so we can study and develop a vaccine. Sin acts in similar ways to a virus. We are susceptible to it, it passes through exposure, it causes suffering, and we become infected. Jesus became our cure, and this is the good news of the Gospel.

Many thousands of years ago, a virus started with one man and one woman; this virus was sin, and Adam and Eve were Patient Zero. From the beginning, God had a rescue plan, a vaccine if you like.

The introduction of sin not only impacted humans, but it changed all forms of life. In similar ways, the Bible informs the physical world "groaned under the weight of sin."[28] The human body has degraded from its original perfect state, and through the generations, our bodies became prone to viruses, bacteria, and disease. Several laws and protocols of the Old Testament deal with social distancing for the benefits of public health[29] and the slowing down of transmissions through bodily fluids. In a time of our global pandemic, we have the opportunity to view these laws and regulations, not in a framework of prohibition from an angry God, or observations of societal structures belonging in their specific context and timeframe, instead, as measures undertaken by a loving God. At a time when human minds could not comprehend the unseen, and the concept of a microscope was beyond even the wisest, God looked out for us. He was in the process of saving us.

Whereas the Jews of old would have to announce in a loud-voice "unclean unclean,"[30] we, the fortunate ones, have healthcare systems to assist with natural viruses and the completed works of Jesus to take away the infection of spiritual sin.

Jesus took the sins of the world into his soul, his spirit, his body—he absorbed the enormity of this weight on the cross. He took the virus of

---

28. Rom 8:19–22 NIV

29. Refer to Lev 13:2–5, 13:31–33, 13:45–46, 14:8, 14:35, Num 5:2–3, 12:14, 31:19, 2 Chr 26:21, Luke 17:12 NIV

30. Lev 13:45 NIV

sin and provided the cure. The challenge humanity faced, through the millennia leading to the birth of Jesus, is we did not understand how viruses spread, and for the millennia following Jesus, we often continue to ignore the spread of sin. The original virus.

Sin, as a spiritual virus, is the most extreme issue humans will need to face. Sin will penetrate and invade the whole person, affecting the body, mind, and soul. And because we are integrated, sin produces symptoms damaging our emotions, relationships, and every part of our lives. It is deadly, and we have no cure outside of Jesus. It is the cause of suffering in our fallen world.

I say sin is spiritual in a sense it is empowered and rooted in the spiritual. If humans consist of only flesh and blood, there would be no need to deal with sin. The animal kingdom has suffered through the result of sin, but the animal kingdom is immune to sin. Because sin is a spiritual virus, it needs a spiritual cure, and this cure came through the completed work of Jesus on the cross. With the eternally defining words, "it is finished," Jesus broke the curse of sin, and through the blood of Jesus, we have received our cleansing.[31] The allegorical vaccine freely administered through the simplest of acts: forgiveness.

Sin is the cause of suffering in our fallen world.

In my journey, I have witnessed much suffering, not mine, but the pain of others from the large-scale refugee crisis in south-east Asia and the middle-east to suffering at the individual level. Life is a great gift, but the circumstances of where life is born will determine the development of this life or will determine the decline of this new life, and in many instances, life will seem anything other than a gift.

Our first child was conceived in West Africa, and it was this expectation of life that changed our world. We were creating a human, and we were adding to the human community, yet in this part of Africa, pain was real, and suffering was on a large scale. There would be another mother just around the corner, down the road, in the next compound who would be passing HIV to their child. Another mother would have difficulties during childbirth resulting in a lack of oxygen to their newborn, giving rise to suffering. Another mother would be raising a child on the street, in an abusive situation. Another mother was giving birth to a baby and needing immediate medical attention, but this medical attention not being available—countless mothers delivering children with no medical attention.

On another occasion in East Timor, I entered the intimate gathering of a family who had lost their son. What made this more poignant was their

---

31. Refer to 1 John 1:7 NIV

son was the same age as my son, and the comparisons of each boys' lives were beyond compare, leaving a profound impression on me.

I was in East Timor to visit projects, and as was my usual practice, I would write up a report for a publication of my experiences and observations. I include a section of this report to highlight this challenging encounter. If for nothing more, to pay honor to a boy who momentarily lived on our precious earth.

The Passing of Augistinho
I do struggle to recall whether Augistinho was the first lifeless body I'd encountered. I'd come across several bodies on the streets of Bangkok without knowing the full extent of their injury.

Along with a nurse from New Zealand, I'd journeyed to the grieving house-hold to offer condolences for the tragic passing of Augistinho, and to bring rice and oil.

Augistinho's home was as humble as it was modest, a simple structure consisting of wood perched on concrete posts. Entering through the small door frame, I delicately navigated past the hand-crafted and infant-sized casket, the casket where Augistinho's body would soon be laid. In silence, I was ushered further into the home, passing the now-vacated cot. Despite it being the middle of the day, the room remained shadowed, taking several moments for my eyes to adjust before making out the shape of Augistinho's small frame presented on a wooden table towards the back of the room. Laid on his back, with feet together and hands placed one on top of the other, his eyes remaining open.

Augistinho was only three, the same age as my youngest. I moved to greet Natalina, but through her desperate wailing, I'm not sure if my stepping forward was well-timed. The only phrases I could speak were "good morning" and "good afternoon," neither appropriate to a grieving mother. Instead, I hesitantly reached out to shake her hand, gave a polite smile, and turned my eyes to the lifeless body laid out before me. Time had momentarily stopped.

Augistinho looked restful and peaceful. He lay just as my three-year-old son would lay for one last kiss before sleep and for me to say a prayer of blessing over his life.

Augistinho will wake no more. His last breath had gone. Could it have been an agonizing breath, labored from the plight of malaria that finally and painstakingly stole his life? Was he held close and tight in the comforting arms of his mother as he slipped away? I don't know.

Lovingly placed on the table next to his body was a single pair of shoes, a few items of modest clothing, and a bag in which I struggled to make out its contents; a few toys, perhaps? I pondered with the singular thought; did this small collection of items represent the totality of his life's possessions?

My thoughts turned to the surplus of toys in my sons' bedroom. I considered how tidying these toys each night might now take on a whole new perspective. At least I had toys to tidy. For Natalina, her mothers' privilege had passed. Natalina was now silent, with eyes desperately empty.

I was later to learn of the terrible fear locals have of seeking medical help in Dili. Worry stemming from the journey still perceived to be fraught with danger but also of the security and the poor state once inside the nation's main hospital. In Dili, in this particular moment in their history, in war's aftermath, hospitals were associated with death and dying, and not health and healing.

This fear perhaps cost the life of a young boy.

It was hard for me to comprehend this fear as I had made the journey to the hospital numerous times over the past week. Yet, I was making this journey without the history of knowing the terror that had torn this country apart.

Augistinho was a casualty of this conflict. He didn't die from a bullet, but he did die as a result of a health service decimated through bombings, lootings, through the loss of medical personnel, of the lingering fear generated through armed conflict, and of a crippled tax base not able to invest in medical infrastructure. Peace is needed to invest in human life. This lack of peace claimed another victim that day.

Observing this solemn gathering of family and friends, I had a deep sense of how Natalina and God were united in their shared grief and heartache over the loss of a child.

God may be accused of not intervening. Yet, he was right there, bringing comfort and peace to the broken-hearted and bringing the assurance that amid despair, we can find hope. I consider how the angels would have observed God wailing alongside the grief-stricken family.

Augistinho's name may not be remembered as an official victim of the violence that had engulfed this tiny nation. Still, I consider every tear shed that day was noticed by God, and I think a solemn silence in heaven may have met the passing of Augistinho.

It was now time to depart, and we left Natalina in her desperate grief and took to the road heading to the now-familiar junction where the road forks. On previous days we'd navigated this fork at a steady pace; today would be different. The fork had become a makeshift military checkpoint, constructed with speed and guarded by a dozen or so relatively young and anxiously alert UN military personnel rapidly responding to the real threat of insurgents moving in from the east to advance on the capital of the nation. As we slowed, smiled, and drifted past, I caught myself reflecting on a life wasted and the role of fear—the saddest event.

The following days had an immense impact on me. Even in my downtime, I felt an agitation of living in a broken world. I took to seeking solace on walks beyond the village borders, but even in the stunning beauty of

East Timor, the echoes of war were ever-present. I watched the sunset over the stunning, pristine white-sand beach of the Banda Sea, and the reality of the environment was once more forced upon me as the now all too familiar beating of a helicopter rotor punctuated this otherwise tranquil but surreal moment. I was no longer alone in this idyllic landscape. Rarely was I alone. The near-constant drone of low flying security helicopters, blades cutting the air, created a surreal security umbrella of wonderment, noise, and a sense of protection. As I swam in the fading light of the day, it was as though I had my private security umbrella just meters above my head.

A strange sense of security had set in. Secure in knowing the choppers are there and fully loaded. Safe knowing UN and military vehicles continually patrol the roads, yet a strange reality that this is happening above and around me for a good reason. No doubt, peace will be realized in East Timor, a new war elsewhere will erupt and capture the headlines. No doubt, the UN will be called upon to deliver peace in another far-flung country. But for now, and through my humble report, I hope to bring remembrance to Augistinho.

My report remains unfinished. I could not bring myself to complete it; it sits on my top shelf, a reminder of the sanctity of life and the challenge of death.

This story, and more besides, enforce my notion that it seems many people are just plain unlucky as to the circumstances in which they are born. Yet, we do need the faith that God celebrates each life born and that God has a perfect plan and an excellent purpose for each new life. Life's defining purpose is to grow into the knowledge of being a child of God, and this knowledge is more than sufficient to carry us through the worst that the world can throw at us. Our challenge is to be appalled at the dreadful living conditions for millions of people while developing community responses to these needs.

Our relationship with God is a covenant relationship, and within this covenant relationship, we do take on board the priorities and concerns of God, as our covenant partner. Jesus came to bring the fullness of life, and we are purposed to deliver this fullness of life. The Bible tells us that we will do more than Jesus[32]. For many years I pondered this promise. More than Jesus? How? Jesus raised people from death. Jesus walked on water. Jesus was crucified and took on the sin, pain, and all the wrongs of this world. Jesus, who rose from the dead. How can we do more than this? And I wonder whether this is numerical and geographical? In the short time Jesus walked on earth, he did not feed the hungry in Asia. He did not meet the needs of

---

32. Refer to John 14:12

people sleeping rough in America. He did not address the issue of freedom in China. Yet, we can, and we do.

This is our purpose.

My picture of God emotionally wailing alongside Natalina may generate an image some become uncomfortable with. Some may consider that God would not notice. Others may deem it more appropriate for God to remain stoic and not to allow his resolve to be engaged by such a human trait as emotions. Yet, Jesus wept over Jerusalem, and we are made in the image of God. Jesus sweated blood on the cross for Augistinho, and through doing so, God has full empathy and complete authority to feel the pain of Augistinho and those who mourned that day.

Some may be troubled in considering God as an emotional God, and some may find it inappropriate for God to be impacted by the actions of our lives. The opposite, an aloof, unattached, and disinterested God, is by far a more fearsome conclusion.

God created us with freewill, and for God to remain committed to humans through our journey of freewill requires God to be impacted as a result. God grieves for us. Because we are made in God's image, parents too grieve at their children's pain.

We can often view life through the prism of a silent God who has accusation after accusation levied at him. Our response to these accusations, combined with God's apparent silence, can have us shying away from God so as not to be co-accused through name association, or to become like Judas and sell him out. Perhaps we become like a commander-in-chief and consider it our duty to fight and to defend his corner. Yet, God continues to not intervene in the way in which we desire while maintaining his long periods of apparent silence. Creating, for his followers, a nervous vacuum in which we can fill this void with our ungrounded theories and our attempts at an explanation. If left unattended, this apparent vacuum generates fear from our experience of disorientation, happening within the complexities of our freedom of choice.

Freewill is one of the hardest facets to comprehend. We see the results of freewill on the news night after night. War. Revenge. Scandal. Politicizing. School shooting. Economic inequality. Other times, an unequal response to an earthquake. Tsunami. Flooding. Draught. COVID-19. At the micro-level, domestic abuse. Child exploitation. Joblessness. Depression. Revenge porn. Lack of hope and purpose. We need to advocate within this environment.

Neglecting this need can lead to disorientation toward God. Similar to the two disciples on the road to Emmaus,[33] confessing, "we had hoped that he was the one."[34]

This man was Jesus.

How many times do I struggle with this same disorientation? "I had hoped that he was the one?" Within the depths of my heart, I do have the surety of Jesus being all that he said he is, yet, it is often on the surface of situations and relationships where this clarity is not always as sure-footed. I say, "I had hoped that this situation would have worked out differently." "If only Jesus could have intervened." My personal why questions adding to our collective history of why questions, pointing towards individual and collective disorientation.

We had hoped he was the one. I had hoped he was the one.

Semblances of this disorientation can creep into our minds revealing the limits of our understanding. We value freedom of choice and lament this freedom of choice when faced with the consequences. We can feel it justifiable for God to intervene actively and curtail the freedom of choice in the lives of individuals. The drunk driver who killed a mother of young children. The disgruntled employee who vents his anger through the barrel of a gun. The leader of an army who unleashes hell on defenseless civilians. The despot who brings a nation to ruin based on a flawed philosophy. The relentless bully. Why could God not have narrowed the definition of freedom for Hitler or Pol Pot?

Prayer bridges this schism where disorientation faces faith. Through prayer, we enter this apparent silence and commune with God and learn of God's heart for humanity, and we learn that God has a heart that's also broken and a heart that also dreams. I draw close to the mind of God through prayer, and in doing so, I learn that God waits. He waits for my initiative. He waits for me to act upon what he has already spoken. He tolerates my personal why questions, often year after year, waiting for me to understand they have previously been answered. It's at this juncture I start to comprehend my role in this silence. He has called me to speak on his behalf and to bring good news and healing to the nations.

My silence in the face of the slave trade now becomes uncomfortable. My silence in the public debate on freedom soon becomes questionable. Silence in the face of cruelty is no longer an option; it is no spiritual act to remain in silence.

---

33. Refer to Luke 24:13–34 NIV
34. Luke 24:21 NIV

When I realize that God has already saved the day and all I need to do is proclaim this, I realize God is waiting on me, waiting for me while tolerating my silence and preoccupation with things that distract—putting up with my ideas on how and when he should act. In an age of instant gratification, I am perhaps losing the ancient practice of patience.

When we view life in the temporal, patience can make little sense. When we consider life in the eternal, patience now takes on a new meaning. Besides laziness and apathy, time is not wasted in an environment where time does not exist.

Through prayer and through gaining the right understanding of God, my state of disorientation becomes my state of wonder through marveling at his awesomeness.

As King David did through the Psalms, I lament my doubt, and I speak my disorientation, and in doing so, I am comforted by God. I do continue to live in this flawed world, and I will continually be impacted through this same imperfect world. However, the difference that makes me flawesome is found in my resolve to believe that I am perfected through Jesus.

The world is desperately awaiting the unveiling of our authentic identity. Until we discover our true identity and to purposefully move away from a self-centric living, while laying down our lives on behalf of others, we will remain by and mostly ineffective in the realm of kingdom advancement bringing societal change.

To tackle the world's problems will need the type of confidence and ambition that can only come from God and the faith that says, "everything is possible."[35] We do need practical solutions to practical problems, and we do have the answers to societal needs. When we pray "thy kingdom come,"[36] and when we "seek first his kingdom,"[37] there is a great responsibility on our behalf to answer the question; what does this kingdom look like in my community? How will the kingdom of God impact societal needs? How will it affect the fair provision of healthcare services and other community needs such as security, homelessness, addictions, crime statistics, abuse, education, and business? How will the kingdom answer the challenge of isolation and loneliness, anxiety, and depression? Isolation is a real challenge in our increasingly connected world, both voluntary and involuntary disengagement.

Followed by the next questions, what is my role?

35. Matt 19:26 NIV
36. Luke 11:2 KJV
37. Matt 6:33 NIV

The Bible remains the most practical of books, and its guidance on how to live life to the fullest is unparalleled. The Bible is not a self-help book as in the genre of self-help books, yet the instruction on how to live is as incomparable as it is complete.

The Bible discusses the two practices of "renewing the mind"[38] and of "taking every thought captive."[39] At first consideration, these practices may seem hard tasks. Yet, they are both necessary, and they are both doable. It is possible to have God speak into our thoughts,[40] and it is possible to have a constant renewing of the mind. As with most learned skills, it does take patience and practice, achieved through the way we live our lives:

- We live with the hope of Jesus
- We are confident in our identity
- We become firmly rooted in Jesus
- We like ourselves, and we rejoice in our weaknesses
- We consider the needs of others before our own, and we give other people the benefit of the doubt
- We live in a constant state of peace with God and peace with each other. We do not worry, and we do not speculate on the negative
- We keep short accounts with each other
- We believe the impossible until it becomes the reasonable
- We are thankful people
- We talk to God about our problems
- We set our eyes on the things of God
- We discern and filter that which would have an influence on our lives
- We think about God
- We put in to practice our faith on a decision by decision basis

Renewing, in its reference to the human mind, is chosen carefully. Renewing validates the creative genius of God in his fashioning of our intricate bodies, where a pre-fall mechanism (the ability for our minds to be renewed) was created, allowing the transformation of the human mind. As if it were born-again.

---

38. Rom 12:2 NIV
39. 2 Cor 10:5 NIV
40. Refer to Rom 12:2, 1 Cor 2:16, Phil 2:13 NIV

I do suggest the protoevangelium, as discussed previously, of Genesis[41] as the first occurrence of the gospel message of Jesus Christ, yet, predating this protoevangelium, God provided humans with this renewal mechanism. The ability of our minds to be renewed and transformed.

Renewed but not rewired. And in doing so, we become. We become the person we are created to be.

---

41. Refer to Gen 3:15 NIV

28

Became. Becoming. Become.

When you have mastered numbers, you will in fact no longer be reading numbers, any more than you read words when reading books. You will be reading meanings.

William Edward Burghardt Du Bois[1]

We Become because of Jesus, who Became.

The perfected life of Jesus allows us to Become. The covenant marriage is a standing example. The covenant of marriage is perfect, yet, the human signatories to this covenant are far from perfect. However, this does not make the covenant marriage imperfect. And this is the relationship God has called us to. A perfected covenant relationship made perfect by God with the complete understanding that the human partner in this covenant will fail time and time again. God knows our inabilities to be perfect, and God chooses to remain perfect, loyal, and fully committed to his covenantal relationship with us.

Even though our identity is no longer defined as being a sinner, our minds succumb to temptation, and our bodies can act accordingly to this temptation—the difference between identity and character. I am no longer a sinner, yet I continue to sin through exposure and character deficiency.

Although I have become, I continue the journey of becoming, and this a journey whereby I transition through salvation.

1. Du Bois, as quoted on Goodreads

29

Progressive Salvation

The important thing is not to stop questioning. Curiosity has its own reason for existence. One cannot help but be in awe when he contemplates the mysteries of eternity, of life, of the marvelous structure of reality. It is enough if one tries merely to comprehend a little of this mystery each day.

ALBERT EINSTEIN[1]

EARLIER, WE DISCUSSED SALVATION as a transactional event and how this transactional event is our liberation. True, however, this does limit the ongoing role of salvation in the disciple's life. Salvation is exceedingly more than being constrained as an individualized and one-dimensional event. It calls us to the center of the community and to help alleviate the problems of this world and to provide God's wisdom into our systems of healthcare, politics, and commerce, extending salvation to the refugee and the slave. To mend broken lives and restore broken families.

Salvation changes our past, impacts our present, and secures our future.

Our past salvation. Our present salvation. Our future salvation.

- We *became* through the past tense of salvation. For the follower of Jesus, this act is now complete

1. Einstein, "Old Man's Advice"

- We are *becoming* through the ongoing and present tense of salvation. Being the transformational journey from that of a follower of Jesus to becoming a disciple
- We *become* through the future tense of salvation, where we look towards the culmination of our complete freedom in fullness, and for eternity.[2]

The future tense of salvation would remove even the temptation of sin, with sin being removed upon entering the perfected covenantal relationship with God in the coming kingdom of Heaven.

Salvation becomes the ongoing work of liberation defining our lives as being freed from the penalty of sin, and this definition is who we are. It is the foundation of our identity. It is through salvation that we become sure of the past and become confident in the future.

The present tense of salvation, the here and now, is exceedingly important in our lives. And how we respond to this present tense will shape our character and impact our behavior. We often fall into the rut of waiting in apathy, frustration, and defeat, rather than thoroughly engaging life in all of its freedom. The challenge we face daily is that of choice. Discipleship is a choice, and Isaiah provides two critical elements in daily making choices:

- To be strong[3]
- To be holy[4]

To be speaks to the heart of identity and emphasizes our involvement and responsibility in our future selves. To be strong and to be holy requires a decision-by-decision commitment.

Whereas the past tense of salvation is unconditional, the experience of ongoing freedom is conditional, primarily influenced by the choices we make. The complete transformation of our lives can only come from God, yet, we do need to submit to this transformational work, and this is a work influenced mainly by our willingness. A willingness to paddle as a follower or our readiness to dive into the deep as a disciple.

---

2. Refer to Rom 5:9–10 NIV
3. Refer to Isa 35:4, Isa 41:6 NIV
4. Refer to Isa 4:3, Isa 58:13, Isa 62:12 NIV

30

Discipleship's Role in Freedom

> *The count moved in his affairs as in a huge net, trying not to believe that he was entangled but becoming more and more so at every step, and feeling too feeble to break the meshes or to set to work carefully and patiently to disentangle them.*
>
> Leo Tolstoy[1]

DISCIPLESHIP BECOMES THE MECHANISM whereby we engage whole-heartedly in a life set free. Alternatively, we choose to neglect our freedom and live a life of compromise and missed opportunities. In this situation, the prison door is open, yet we choose to remain in the cell and compromise the promise of entering a life of significance and wonder. We still see Jesus from the barrenness of the prison cell but fail to journey with him, and we fail to grasp the meaning of life in its entirety.

After enduring 27-years of imprisonment for standing against the injustice of Apartheid, Mandela had the strength and wisdom to reflect:

> As I walked out the door toward the gate that would lead to freedom, I knew if I didn't leave my bitterness behind, I'd still be in prison.[2]

---

1. Tolstoy, *War and Peace*
2. Mandela, as quoted on Goodreads

To fully engage life requires the transformation from a follower of Jesus to a disciple, achieved through the renewing of the mind. The renewing of the mind is needed to eradicate the dirt of life, the junk of habits, and the grime of attitudes that can become deeply anchored and entrenched in our soul. In one sense, we are born-again while still needing a lifestyle of cleansing, and this becomes the reason why the disciple can struggle through life with sin.

Sin cannot be tamed. We cannot find a peaceful way to live with sin, and we cannot control sin, or use internal strength and determination to nullify the impact of sin, nor can we manage sin. Resolutions and willpower alone will not overcome our ongoing battle against sin. Discipline is necessary, but discipline outside of a relationship with God will ultimately fail, and at the heart of discipline is pure love, the kind of love that we crave. Still, we will only truly experience this in the fullness of heaven. We've often and wrongly used discipline in the past to set a standard whereby we can compare and contrast the holiness of each other. We read of this in the gospels where Jesus accused the religious leaders of setting a rule that no human could attain.[3] The religious leaders were using scripture to implement observable measures, whereas Jesus came to bring love and to bring freedom from the power of sin.

Sin is dealt with through the completed works of Jesus, and our willing alignment to Jesus's finished works.

Although sin does not need to have a hold on us, we are impacted by the consequence of sin every day. We can choose to make sin a travel-partner, and at first, it may seem tolerable and most likely enjoyable for a fraction of time, for if sin were not pleasant, our battle against sin would be easy.

The nature of sin is to tempt and to provide a thoroughly degraded version of satisfaction. When this degraded version of satisfaction becomes all we know, we return to that which we have become accustomed to. By doing so, we enter the downward spiral of a longed-for pleasure being replaced with the unsettling and destructive nature of grief, pain, sorrow, and shame. At the same time, we find dissatisfaction and growing frustration as each level of sin reveals its emptiness and broken promises. A great sadness casts a long shadow on our soul, and we respond to this shadow through turning to Jesus or through turning to jealousy, self-help, and unhappiness.

No matter how hard we try, however, or how many programs we subscribe to, we are unable to redeem ourselves. History proves this through the narrative of the Old Testament, and in our personal lives. Those times where we've made resolutions and commitments only to find we break them, we

---

3. Refer to Matt 23:1–7, Luke 11:52, John 8:1–11 NIV

lose interest or swap one modification for another. We cannot escape the reality of living in our flawed state needing redemption.

Our behavior will get us to a particular place, but our behavior will not get us to our desired destination. While it remains true that behavioral change is the mark of a follower of Jesus, behavioral change is not our goal; instead, it is a much-needed consequence of our decisions.

God isn't looking for compliance through behavioral modification. He's looking for heart connection and transformation. Our character should portray a liberated person with the confidence to promote life in every situation and to have a level of braveness to consider personal sacrifice as an at-times necessity. The disciple needs to hold things loosely and to be ready to use their confidence, generated from their perfected identity as a means to further the values and principles of the kingdom of God on earth. To learn to act as freed people. To learn to think as freed people.

Perhaps the most significant inhibitor to this lifestyle is to believe we are defined by our character (that can remain involved in a sin) rather than being defined by our identity (no longer a sinner). While our character can fail us as we stumble through poor behavior, toxic ideas, and poor decisions, our identity need not stumble. James writes of the working of a contrite heart that will see our transformation:

> So let God work his will in you. Yell a loud *no* to the Devil and watch him scamper. Say a quiet *yes* to God and he'll be there in no time. Quit dabbling in sin. Purify your inner life. Quit playing the field. Hit bottom, and cry your eyes out. The fun and games are over. Get serious, really serious. Get down on your knees before the Master; it's the only way you'll get on your feet.[4]

Over recent history, some practice has focused on behavioral modification as opposed to renewal—prohibition versus freedom. Prohibition without the real and tangible hope of a brighter future rarely works. This does not give license to anarchy, though. Societies do need a benchmark for behavior, and these are documented and empowered through our laws. Without such, we would soon learn a state of anarchy does anything but build a society and develop the populace. Following a nation's civil breakdown or the establishment of a new nation, a priority is for just laws to be written and enacted. Of the most unsafe places in our world is to live in a lawless society, where rival leaders raise their flags to impose their priorities. We see this in the landscape of the Old Testament.

The Law of God, viewed through the safe and protected framework of modern societies, can lead to angst and misinformed opinion. God

---

4. Jas 4:8–10, MSG

delivered the Law into a context of slavery, child sacrifice, shocking practices, and corruption. The Law of God was revolutionary. It advocated for human rights and initiated a judicial system to the degree that society could handle. Messaging was clear; consequences were known. The Law was not a half-hearted measure, nor based on human prejudice or bias. It removed the danger that exists between knowing and not knowing and deciding to act regardless.

Prohibitive laws are needed in our fallen world.

Consider the prolific murderer. Society needs not to be subject to this person while their mind remains in a state of collapse. The government has the responsibility of protection, and as such, prohibitive detention is necessary. Yet, even in this restrictive environment, liberation is available to the worst of our kind. Denying such liberation would add terms and conditions to the love of God and the completed work of Jesus on the cross. Many inmates find salvation in their restrictive environment, perhaps as the concepts of freedom and condemnation have become real to them. The hope of a savior coming to fling wide the prison gates and to set the captive free[5] takes on significant meaning to a soul behind bars.

I once spoke, on an island of breathtaking beauty, to a group of prisoners on this topic. Being mindful of the correctional officers' attentive ears I spoke the message that despite their present circumstances, they have as much right to the renewal of their minds as I do, and the freedom of their soul as to any other. That God's kingdom knows no prison cell besides the prison cells Jesus came to open. I continued that we are not hard-wired, and the renewal of the mind is the only way to live. The simple message being despite our lot-in-life, we can make this lot the best version of life that we can. Of how Jesus wants to become our advocate and liberator, and our mind can be free despite societal restriction.

Liberated people with liberated thinking.

---

5. Refer to Luke 4:18 NIV

31

The Secret Life of Humans

The people are in effect living a reduced version of their former lives. Instead of raging against their destiny they have made things tolerable by lowering their standards.

GEORGE ORWELL[1]

THE OLD TESTAMENT CAN be viewed as very practical, very outward, and physical, with the conclusion that what happened in the material is a reflection of what happens in the spiritual of the New Testament. To a certain degree, this analysis has worth, but it remains an incomplete analysis. God has always desired heart to heart connection, and this has always been the case. We need to look no further than to the countless examples within the Old Testament of God's care for a human. The Psalms attributed to David, provide an intimate glimpse of this heart to heart connection.

The law is a significant presence in the Old Testament, yet we do well to consider that the law is not a facsimile of God. It's not a document that represents the fullness of God. The law was for our benefit and not God's.[2] In Psalm 19, David writes, "The law of the Lord is perfect."[3] Further, in Psalm 19, David provides the ground on which this claim is made "By them your

---

1. Orwell, *The Road to Wigan Pier*.
2. Refer to Deut 4:40, 6:17–18, 7:12–14, 10:13 NIV
3. Ps 19:7 NIV

servant is warned; in keeping them is great reward."[4] The perfection of the law was in its ability to warn and to provide.

The law became our security through the millennium leading to the birth of Jesus. On a time-line, the law represents just a portion of the Old Testament period, but an essential portion of time nonetheless. It showed humans how to maximize their life within a defined framework. It could explain, with perfect clarity, the workings of the cause and effect relationship between humanity and their choices. To not follow the law would result in disease and self-inflicted curses.[5] To follow the law would result in life.[6]

We can become challenged when discovering the specific details and practice of many of the hundreds of laws covering a detailed explanation of how to live life. In our twenty-first century framework of understanding, this is a reasonable challenge if not taken in the fullness of its context. At the heart of the law was protection for Israel and the blessing of the nations. The security of the individual and the welfare of the downcast. We do not doubt the law of gravity that determines the consequence of falling from a great height, yet, we rebel against the laws of God that require us to love our neighbor, and to warn of impending heartache if we break the relationship.

The law was evident, and it was highly visible.

Take the example of Miriam. Moses's and Aaron's sister, a prophetess, and leader of Israel.[7] Miriam, as a leader, was instrumental in the liberation of Israel from Egypt.[8] Along with her brother Aaron, Miriam criticized Moses for taking a Cushite wife.[9] This action displeased the Lord, and Miriam's skin became leprous, and in line with the law concerning leprosy,[10] Miriam was confined to the outskirts of the camp for seven days.[11] This isolation was a highly visible position for Miriam to find herself in. Society, community, friends, and neighbors had no shadow of a doubt over Miriam's current state of affairs. She was *unclean* and isolated. The law of the Old Testament shines a spotlight on sin, and society was aware of each other's sin. All saw. All knew.

Whereas sin in the Old Testament was atoned for publicly, our sin can remain secret. This secrecy, however, becomes detrimental to us and

4. Refer to Ps 19:11 NIV
5. Refer to Deut 28:15–36 NIV
6. Refer to Deut 28:1–14 NIV
7. Refer to Mic 6:4 NIV
8. Refer to Mic 6:4 NIV
9. Refer to Num 12:1 NIV
10. Refer to Lev 13 NIV
11. Refer to Num 12:15 NIV

harmful to the broader community. We carry secrets of guilt, shame, and regret for decades, and this does weigh us down in every aspect of our lives. It can influence our diet, our emotional stability, relationships, and can impact our children where secrecy has the potential to generate generational hurdles, and leave internal scars only God can see, but others can be impacted by. Newspapers and family history highlight stories of secrets finally revealed on a death-bed, and this gives no more unambiguous indication that the act of confession is for our benefit.

The New Testament, in many ways, strengthens the ethics and morality of the law:

- Do not murder becomes do not hate[12]
- Do not commit adultery becomes do not lust[13]
- Do not covet becomes the giving away of our coat to the needy[14]

These three pillars of Jesus's Sermon on the Mount[15] sees Jesus launch a counter-cultural way of life. It was an attack on the secret life that generates hatred, greed, and lust. On the surface, perhaps, there seems less evidence in the Old Testament of the law governing internal thoughts; instead, it highlights the actions resulting from these thoughts. The Sermon on the Mount goes to the heart of life and becomes essential as a roadmap towards perfection.

Such is the power of its message. The Sermon on the Mount is honored, highly respected, and the foundation for living for over two thousand years. It is considered one of the greatest speeches of all time. Authors, politicians, philosophers, and Presidents bring honor to these words. I include a select few of these quotes to drive home its prominence.

In the words of Franklin D. Roosevelt:

> No greater blessing could come to our land today than a revival of the spirit of religion. I doubt if there is any problem in the world today—social, political, or economic—that would not find happy solution if approached in the spirit of the Sermon on the Mount.[16]

Mohandas Karamchan Gandhi:

---

12. Refer to Matt 5:21–22 NIV
13. Refer to Matt 5:27–28 NIV
14. Refer to Matt 5:40 NIV
15. Refer to Matt 5, 6, 7 NIV
16. Roosevelt, *Public Papers of the Presidents*

If then I had to face only the Sermon on the Mount and my own interpretation of it, I should not hesitate to say, 'O yes, I am a Christian'.[17]

Oswald Chambers:

The Sermon on the Mount is not a set of principles to be obeyed apart from identification with Jesus Christ. The Sermon on the Mount is a statement of the life we will live when the Holy Spirit is getting his way with us.[18]

Philip Yancey:

Thunderously, inarguably, the Sermon on the Mount proves that before God we all stand on level ground: murderers and temper-throwers, adulterers and lusters, thieves and coveters. We are all desperate, and that is in fact the only state appropriate to a human being who wants to know God. Having fallen from the absolute ideal, we have nowhere to land but in the safety net of absolute grace.[19]

For freedom of humanity to be realized, it needs to be freedom to the whole person, including our thought life. Society may celebrate lust, and purposefully agitate for the demonstration of frustration for the sake of a social media upload or a reality television show, but this is not freedom. It's merely a misguided and weak form of entertainment. Jesus came to liberate the secret life, and the New Testament addresses how to live in this new reality.

Freedom from all that suppresses is now possible and attainable. Yet, freedom is not static. Constant spiritual vigilance assures ground gained in our lives is not given up at the slightest lure of alternatives promoting their empty promises. We see this need for spiritual awareness and the lure of temptation perhaps no better than the stories of the kings of old.

---

17. Netland, *Christianity and Religious Diversity*
18. Chambers, *The Psychology of Redemption*
19. Yancey, *The Jesus I Never Knew*

32

Lessons from the Lives of Ancient Kings

The Seven Social Sins are:
Wealth without work.
Pleasure without conscience.
Knowledge without character.
Commerce without morality.
Science without humanity.
Worship without sacrifice.
Politics without principle.

FREDERICK LEWIS DONALDSON[1]

THE HALF-MILLENNIA PERIOD COVERING the Kingdoms of Israel and Judah provides deep insight from the reign of King Saul through to the divided kingdom's captivities in Assyria and Babylon. It's a period offering a wealth of understanding, as to our journey of discipleship observed through five key phases:

- The kingdom is united (Saul, (Ish-bosheth), David, Solomon))[2]

---

1. From a sermon given by Frederick Lewis Donaldson in Westminster Abbey, London, on March 20, 1925

2. The Kingdom reaches the heights of its power under King David (1010–970 BC) and King Solomon (970–930 BC)

- The revolt by ten tribes[3]
- The kingdom divided into Israel and Judah[4]
- The two kingdoms taken into exile[5]
- The kingdoms are reunited[6]

A rich period of writing, offering a great depth of wisdom. The period providing the world with the Books of Wisdom, and the Books of History. Many are familiar with timeless lines such as; "Yea, though I walk through the valley of the shadow of death,"[7] "Meaningless! Meaningless! . . . everything is Meaningless,"[8] "There is a time for everything under the sun,"[9] "For unto us a Child is born."[10] All scribed during this period.

It details the lives of 43 men and one woman[11] who rose to the throne of a united kingdom of Israel, and the subsequently divided kingdoms of Israel and Judah. These writings discuss their triumphs and their failings, their entrusted advisors and those who would seek them harm, the word of the Lord through the prophets, the rise and fall of dynasties, kingdoms, and rulers while providing biblical principles to live by. Being the most read book in the world[12] their lives have become both famous and infamous for varying reasons.

The Bible provides a summary of the lives of each of the Kings. In some instances, this summary is the most fleeting of mentions (for example, King Pekahiah[13] and King Shallum).[14] Whereas, for King David, King Saul, and King Solomon, we are provided with a greater depth of insight; personal and intimate at times. Some kings regarded as being good, while other kings considered as being evil, and the narrative captures the change in some of their lives from starting well but finishing poorly.

3. Addressed in 1 Kgs 12 NIV; Judah & Benjamin stayed loyal to the House of David
4. Addressed in the exilic books; Daniel and Esther
5. Addressed in the exilic books; Daniel and Esther
6. Addressed in postexilic books; Ezra, Nehemiah, Haggai, Zechariah, and Malachi
7. Ps 23:4 KJV
8. Eccl 1:2 NIV, abridged
9. Eccl 3:1, 16 NIV abridged
10. Isa 9:6 NIV
11. Athaliah, 2 Kgs 11 NIV
12. Source: The 10 Most Read Books in the World, Jennifer Polland, Business Insider, 27 December 2012
13. Refer to 2 Kgs 15:23–26 NIV
14. Refer to 2 Kgs 15: 13–16 NIV

Often, a general synopsis is provided for each King, an insight to their lineage, their more significant accomplishments, usually an appraisal of how they dealt with the high ground during their reign, while informing of their righteousness or their evil. Besides Kings Saul, David and Solomon, two Kings stand as benchmark Kings: King Asa, who pleased God and King Jeroboam, who did not please God. These Kings become a type of standard to understand the lives of all other Kings.

Numbers of principles help us learn from the lives of the Kings, particularly in understanding our response to the Lordship of Christ:

- God strongly advised Israel against elevating a human to the place reserved for God. This warning was ignored, and a monarchical system formed. God respected and redeemed this choice by allowing Jesus to be born through this lineage. Likewise, we are provided with specific warning as to the danger of placing idols on the high ground of our lives that is reserved for God
- Where an earthly father has been less than a good role model, we do not automatically replicate this father. A principle we see repeated through the lives of the Kings of Israel and Judah
- When we do wrong, we can repent, and God will restore
- Whereas the Kings had prophets speak into their lives, and the example of predecessors to help guide them; we now have the Holy Spirit living within us to act and guide, and the perfect example of Jesus (as King and Lord) as to how to live

These lessons from the lives of ancient kings become invaluable in the journey of discipleship, and the role of idols has perhaps no better example than through the period of the Kings.

33

The Role of the Idol

What is an idol? It is anything more important to you than God, anything that absorbs your heart and imagination more than God, anything you seek to give you what only God can give.

Timothy Keller[1]

Traveling several thousand years back to a time of ancient Kings, we learn of King Solomon. Upon his ascension to the throne, King Solomon inherited a vast kingdom. His father, King David, had ensured his success,[2] and a progression marked the transition from father to son from bloodshed to peace.[3] Peace was established, and the Kingdom primed to develop. David desired to provide for the future of the kingdom. This ambition saw vast supply chain networks, and agreements with neighboring nations to assist in the construction of the temple.[4] Over seven years, the temple was completed,[5] and over an additional number of years, other grandiose structures[6] took their place within a strengthening and confident Jerusalem. A boom time of rapid growth and the elevation of Jerusalem in its status.

1. Keller, *Counterfeit Gods*
2. Refer to 1 Kgs 1: 28–40, 1 Chr 28, 1 Chr 22 NIV
3. Refer to 1 Chr 22:7–10 NIV
4. Refer to 1 Kgs 5: 1–13 NIV
5. Refer to 1 Kgs 6:38 NIV
6. Refer to 1 Kgs 9:10 NIV

The life of King Solomon, however, is an uncomfortable case-study in human activity, from a man who had it all to a man who became plagued by his lifestyle choices. He is a man who flirted with danger and allowed many distractions to compete for the high ground in his life.

Over the following pages, we'll consider the principles we do learn from King Solomon and his life.

His early years had started favorably, and Solomon is perhaps best known for his wisdom;[7] wisdom considered to be beyond compare as captured through two stories.

In the first, we meet two women and two babies. The women shared living quarters, and during one particular night, one woman rolled over, resulting in the baby's unfortunate death. The next morning the woman claimed the living baby to be hers. The case was brought before Solomon, and his decree was met with great admiration for his wisdom.[8]

The second story tells of the fame of Solomon's wisdom. The Bible narrative reveals how the Queen of Sheba traveled to meet with King Solomon.[9] In one sense, she was curious as to the validity of the claims she had heard. Still, quite possibly, this was to be a meeting of commercial and political importance due to the trade routes and geopolitical alliances of the region. The narrative suggests how overcame she was through the wisdom she had encountered:

> And when the queen of Sheba had seen all the wisdom of Solomon, the house that he had built, the food of his table, the seating of his officials, and the attendance of his servants, their clothing, his cupbearers, and his burnt offerings which he offered at the house of the LORD, there was no more breath in her. And she said to the king, "The report was true which I heard in my own land of your words and of your wisdom, but I did not believe the reports until I came and my own eyes had seen it. And, behold, the half was not told me. Your wisdom and prosperity surpass the report which I heard."[10]

Despite all that he had, wisdom, provision, legacy, and personal visitations from God, Solomon fell victim to the desires of his heart, and his fall from grace was stunning not only in its depth but also in its gravity.

---

7. Refer to 1 Kgs 10:23–24 NIV
8. Refer to 1 Kgs 3:16–28 NIV
9. Refer to 1 Kgs 10 NIV
10. 1 Kgs 10:4–9 ESV

The narrative of Genesis allows us to consider there is just the one tree that Adam and Eve were forbidden to eat from,[11] and their curiosity failed them. They had been given explicit instruction.[12] Likewise, King Solomon had a clear definition of the limits of his power and as to the decisions to avoid. Unfortunately for Solomon, he flirted with this danger and suffered a significant consequence. Whereas Adam and Eve had taken a piece of fruit, King Solomon had harvested the crop.

Although the dangers of establishing a kingly dynasty had been warned against by God,[13] we can learn how God continued to work within this limiting human framework. In seeking an earthly King, Israel had fallen to the demands of the inherent human flaw of comparison, the devastating defect that says, "I am not satisfied with my life. I want more."

As a fledgling nation, Israel was experiencing a heightened sense of anxiousness as to the observed shifts in human forms of government happening within their geopolitical region. They responded with the desire for a King, the desire to be led by a strong-man. Previously, God had warned Israel against such demands, and God had provided clear insight as to the changes the nation would experience should they choose a King with an unchecked heart. God's instruction was unambiguous on this; there will be consequences if you elevate a human to a position of power and authority higher than any person is equipped to handle.

God provided all that Israel had ever needed. Nonetheless, Israel ignored God's warnings, doubted his provision, and they pursued more; this pursuit originated in their perceived state of deficiency. Likewise, this ancient concept of desire and lack remains a powerful force today. It is often a repeated theme in our lives. We want more.

The following highlights God's instruction and King Solomon's response

God's instruction:

> The king, moreover, must not acquire great numbers of horses for himself or make the people return to Egypt to get more of them, for the Lord has told you, "You are not to go back that way again.[14]

Solomon's response:

---

11. Refer to Gen 2:17 NIV
12. Refer to Gen 2:17 NIV
13. Refer to 1 Sam 8 NIV
14. Deut 17:16 NIV

THE ROLE OF THE IDOL 163

> Solomon accumulated chariots and horses; he had fourteen hundred chariots and twelve thousand horses.[15]
> Solomon's horses were imported from Egypt.[16]

God's instruction:

> He must not take many wives, or his heart will be led astray.[17]

Solomon's response:

> King Solomon, however, loved many foreign women besides Pharaoh's daughter—Moabites, Ammonites, Edomites, Sidonians and Hittites. They were from nations about which the Lord had told the Israelites, "You must not intermarry with them, because they will surely turn your hearts after their gods."[18]

Further,

> He had seven hundred wives of royal birth and three hundred concubines.[19]

The marrying of seven hundred women from royal heritage speaks of the political might of King Solomon and of how far his political persuasion penetrated: extending into 700 royal courts and Kingdoms within the region. The acquisition of 700 royal wives perhaps speaks more to political maneuvering and influence as it does to singularly highlighting his sexual desire.

God's instruction:

- "He must not accumulate large amounts of silver and gold."[20]

Solomon's response:

- "King Solomon was greater in riches and wisdom than all the other kings of the earth."[21]

- "The weight of the gold that Solomon received yearly was 666 talents."[22]

---

15. 2 Kgs 10:26 NIV
16. 1 Kgs 10:28 NIV
17. Deut 17:17 NIV
18. 1 Kgs 11:1–2 NIV
19. 2 Kgs 11:3 NIV
20. Deut 17:17 NIV
21. 1 Kgs 10:23 NIV
22. 1 Kgs 10:14 NIV

- "King Solomon made two hundred large shields of hammered gold."[23]
- "He also made three hundred small shields of hammered gold."[24]
- "Then the king made a great throne covered with ivory and overlaid with fine gold."[25]
- "Year after year, everyone who came brought a gift—articles of silver and gold, robes, weapons and spices, and horses and mules."[26]

King Solomon accumulated wealth on an unprecedented scale through successfully developing four primary revenue streams:

> Commerce—a fleet of ships[27] commissioned to open up trading routes and develop trading partners

Shortly after the birth of Jesus, the Jewish scholar and historian, Titus Flavius Josephus wrote of this historical period:

> for the King had many ships which lay upon the sea of Tarsus, these he commanded to carry out all sorts of merchandise unto the remotest nations, by the sale of which silver and gold were brought to the king, and a great quantity of ivory, and Ethiopians, and apes; and they finished their voyage, going and returning, in three years' time.[28]
>
> Gifts—common practice of the day would see Kings, rulers, and dignitaries lavish gifts upon those they sought counsel with. We read of this in the case of The Queen of Sheba[29] and the practice of others.[30]
>
> Tributes—King Solomon acquired much wealth from tributes pouring in from kingdoms and nations within his sphere of influence.[31] Whether these tributes were purely voluntary and offered through a sense of admiration, or they were in exchange for favorable relationships and to serve national interests and

---

23. 1 Kgs 10:16 NIV
24. 1 Kgs 10:17 NIV
25. 1 Kgs 10:18 NIV
26. 1 Kgs 10:25 NIV
27. Refer to 1 Kgs 9:26–28, 10:22–23 NIV
28. Josephus, *The Works of Flavius Josephus*
29. Refer to 1 Kgs 10:10 NIV
30. Refer to 1 Kgs 10:25 NIV
31. Refer to 1 Kgs 10:14–15, 24–25 NIV

to provide security, or whether expected through the acknowledged superiority of King Solomon, would be a case-by-case study.

Whatever the motivation and the level of persuasion needed to secure these tributes, they continued to pour into the Kingdom, significantly increasing the wealth of King Solomon.

Taxation—we read the story of Rehoboam,[32] the son of King Solomon, and of how the tribes reached out to Rehoboam regarding the heavy tax burdens that Solomon had placed over them.[33] Although taxation is a common form of raising funds, it would appear through this encounter that the tax King Solomon had put on his subjects had become burdensome.

It is no doubt that King Solomon was rich. Just how abundant remains debated; we can conclude, however, with some level of confidence as to specific aspects of his wealth by using today's standards. In just considering his gold, we can estimate his annual income from gold alone to over one billion US dollars;[34] one further estimate puts the combined wealth of King Solomon as being $2.1 trillion.[35]

There is to be no doubt as to the wealth of King Solomon, and the Bible narrative continues with further insight:

> All King Solomon's goblets were gold, and all the household articles in the Palace of the Forest of Lebanon were pure gold. Nothing was made of silver, because silver was considered of little value in Solomon's days.[36]

And again,

> The king made silver as common in Jerusalem as stones, and cedar as plentiful as sycamore-fig trees in the foothills.[37]

Years earlier, and before entering the Promised Land, God had spoken with similar insight and instruction. As with the case above, Solomon's response is provided after each direction, where time and time again, King Solomon flouted his wisdom.

God's instruction:

32. Refer to 1 Kgs 12 NIV
33. Refer to 1 Kgs 12:4 NIV
34. Source: https://www.biblestudy.org/basicart/how-rich-was-solomon.html
35. Source: https://www.practicalbusinessideas.com/king-solomon-wealth-net-worth/
36. 1 Kgs 10:21 NIV
37. 1 Kgs 10:27 NIV

- "Obey what I command you today. I will drive out before you the Amorites, Canaanites, Hittites, Perizzites, Hivites and Jebusites."[38]
- "Be careful not to make a treaty with those who live in the land where you are going, or they will be a snare among you."[39]
- "Break down their altars, smash their sacred stones and cut down their Asherah poles."[40]
- "Do not worship any other god, for the LORD, whose name is Jealous, is a jealous God."[41]

Solomon's response:

- "his wives turned his heart after other gods, and his heart was not fully devoted to the LORD his God."[42]
- "He followed Ashtoreth the goddess of the Sidonians, and Molek the detestable god of the Ammonites."[43]

God's instruction:

- "And when you choose some of their daughters as wives for your sons and those daughters prostitute themselves to their gods, they will lead your sons to do the same."[44]

Solomon's response.

Besides Rehoboam, we are given little insight into Solomon's children. What we know of Rehoboam is how he followed his father's footsteps in lacking complete trust in God, an indulgence in pleasure, and taking eighteen wives and sixty concubines.[45] Unlike his father, however, Rehoboam married within the lineage of David,[46] and his children appear to be more noteworthy[47] than the undisclosed number of children from Solomon's 1,000 wives and concubines.

God's instruction:

38. Exod 34:11 NIV
39. Exod 34:12 NIV
40. Exod 34:13 NIV
41. Exod 34:14 NIV
42. 1 Kgs 11:4 NIV
43. 1 Kgs 11:5 NIV
44. Exod 34:16 NIV
45. Refer to 2 Chr 11:21 NIV
46. Refer to 2 Chr 11:18 NIV
47. Refer to 2 Chr 11: 18–23 NIV

- "Do not make any idols."[48]

Solomon's response:

> Solomon built a high place for Chemosh the detestable god of Moab, and for Molek the detestable god of the Ammonites. He did the same for all his foreign wives, who burned incense and offered sacrifices to their gods.[49]

Solomon had set a new standard for grandiose displays of personal deficiency, subjected himself to unprecedented disorientation towards God, and ventured towards remarkable wavering in his trust of God. We can read from the Psalms of how his father, too, suffered disorientation towards God and had his share of faults. The defining difference, however, is whereas Solomon had great wisdom, besides fleeting passages,[50] we do not learn much as to the state of his heart. David did not have his son's wisdom, but Solomon did not have his father's undivided heart after God. The crux of the matter. King David became a standard by which future kings of Judah and Israel would be judged in light of the position of their hearts. Solomon's wisdom was not to become such a benchmark.

Solomon chased empty promises as he increasingly built his personal life and shaped his kingly role on a lust for power, authority, wealth, and greed. Yet, even during Solomon's rebellion against the ways of God, God remained constant as to his methods: God initiated warnings with increasing resolve, but these warnings were not immediate, not totally, and not forever.

We read of three adversaries (Hadad the Edomite, Rezon the son of Eliadah, and Jeroboam the son of Nebat)[51] who challenged King Solomon. These adversaries provided the opportunity for Solomon to return to God wholeheartedly. No doubt, Solomon, by this juncture of his life, was without daily intimate communion with God. He may have followed ritual practice and dressed and acted in ways to support this façade, but his heart was hijacked, and his mind had become distracted. God, through his grace, used these three adversaries to bring destruction to the pathways of King Solomon, but not for the end of King Solomon.

Solomon was to be the last king to rule a united kingdom of Israel before it's division to the northern kingdom and southern kingdom.

---

48. Exod 34:17 NIV
49. 1 Kgs 11:7 NIV
50. Refer to 1 Kgs 11:1–8 NIV
51. Refer to 1 Kgs 11:14–38 NIV

As was the case with the three adversaries that arose against King Solomon, similarities can be observed in our lives; God will look to remove the things that destroy us, but he is never looking for the opportunity to destroy us.

He does not give us sickness. He healed our disease.

He does not kill us. He died so we can live.

God does not isolate us. He formed us for relationship.

Should I doubt these statements, then I base my belief on a poor understanding of God. Yet, the mind of collective-humanity, in many instances, is against God, and this leads to the growing collective narrative that God is against us. The nature of God, however, is for us. The Jesus I have come to know welcomes the refugee and chooses to spend time with people who were considered sinners[52] by society at large and by the religious leaders.

God is called many things, some honorable, some dishonorable, yet, he cannot be called inconsistent in his warnings and motivation—the prosperity of the individual and the betterment of society. This consistency, aligned with his eternal love for us, would see the concern of God, bridge the schism of the Testaments to be taught by Jesus, and repeated by the apostles. For this reason, the study of the life of a king from ancient times provides valuable principles for our living. Do we live under God's grace, or do we chase idols?

Beggaring the question, in the twenty-first century, what is an idol? Followed by, when does that thing cross an invisible threshold to become an idol? Perhaps it is best summarised with four statements:

- If I have that, then my life will have security
- If I achieve that, then my life will be significant
- If I do that, then my name will have the status I seek
- If I experience that, then my life will find satisfaction

Identifying "that" in these four statements, combined with the heart attitude, is the forming of our idol. The strength of this idol is found in its hold on us should it be removed, or we begin to experience its deficiency, leading to growing anxiety.

The question of when something becomes an idol can best be expressed as the point it starts to have power over us—ranging from a slight annoyance when something is taken away, through to a severe response.

Money is necessary, and we need money, and money is not an idol. However, when we compromise our values and God's principles to keep or

---

52. Refer to Mark 2:13–17 NIV

gain money, then we have given money a spiritual power. Or, when we have little money, we can exchange trust and faith in God for anxiety and fear, and money has become a power over us. Similar to the pursuit of status, a career, obsession with a person, or lustful and coveting desires for people, product, or pleasure. History shows neither stimuli nor substitution can adequately fill the void we experience.

Today, we can study the life of King Solomon as one who strayed very far from the promise of his life, and through this study, we glean principles to help in our walk. Whereas Solomon had the wisdom of God, we now have the example set by Jesus, and we have the fullness of the spirit of God living in us.

Rarely does a follower of Jesus arise one morning with a clear objective to reject their lifestyle. It is more common for this fall to be gradual; to fall one step at a time. The type of graduality that can quietly go unnoticed or easily ignored, or viewed as a minor error of judgment. The kind of graduality that would see a large ship make a 180 degree turn over the space of several nautical miles, turning just one small degree at a time. I would suggest this was the case for King Solomon, that he did not suffer from one epic fall. Instead, he made one small compromise at a time, and each compromise allowed for his guard to lower just that little bit more. And while God receded from the high ground of his life, countless idols were waiting to be acknowledged and receive their empowerment. Unguarded moments accumulated in his life, and would ultimately define his life and his rulership.

King Solomon's life appeared as destroyed from the inside out, similar in pattern to the condition of the heart rot fungus. A fungus that attacks trees, ultimately rendering it structurally unsound. Like secret sin, heart rot is unnoticed as it takes hold of the tree and works its destruction below the surface where evidence is finally seen through visible growths on the outside of the bark. Similar to humans grappling with unguarded and secret sin that tends to present itself externally, at some point in its destructive journey.

For Solomon, it was wealth, power, and greed that contributed to his downfall. For each of us, our temptation may look very similar; wealth, power, and greed, and each of us will have differing levels of victory over the temptations that come our way. Yet, we are never alone. The New Testament provides insight as to how to discern and identify these opposing forces:

> Each person is tempted when they are dragged away by their own evil desire and enticed.[53]

---

53. Jas 1:13–14 NIV

Continuing, Peter addresses the role of the devil in this dragging away:

> Your enemy the devil prowls around like a roaring lion looking for someone to devour.[54]

Nonetheless, it does remain of utmost importance to continually remember how this battle is not a physical battle between people. It is a spiritual battle:

> Against the rulers, against the authorities, against the powers of this dark world and against the spiritual forces of evil in the heavenly realms.[55]

We become disempowered and vulnerable when we let our imaginations become compromised. Or, we allow an elevated opinion of our status to develop. In these instances, we allow our lives to be guided by:

> The lust of the flesh, the lust of the eyes, and the pride of life.[56]

These select passages are direct. The challenge for many is living in societies growing confident in their rejection of our faith. John explains this well:

> If you belonged to the world, it would love you as its own. As it is, you do not belong to the world, but I have chosen you out of the world. That is why the world hates you.[57]

In an increasingly intolerant world, the peculiarness of our faith will be highlighted all the more.[58] And as our peculiarity shines, we need to make sure it shines bright with selfless love demonstrated through brave friendship and relentless charity. To a watching world, the follower of Jesus may look strange and odd, just as our priorities and values often do look strange and odd in a world of shifting ideas and evolving values.

To fully live is to engage with God fully. To fully engage with God requires the giving up of self-centric rights and the removal of idols that have been permitted to claim the high ground in our lives. But, for the purpose of what?

Why would God desire our hearts?[59]

---

54. 1 Pet 5:8 NIV
55. Eph 6:12 NIV
56. 1 John 2:16 NIV
57. John 15:19 NIV
58. Refer to 1 Pet 2:9 KJV
59. Refer to Prov 23:26 NIV

Why would God desire each of us to love him with our whole heart?[60]

Besides being a life-defining human organ, the heart symbolically represents the completeness and fullness of our life. In one sense, Jesus has not taken residence in our human beating heart; instead, the heart is indicative of a person's center. It represents who we are, the deepest part of a person. To say "Jesus lives in my heart," "I've welcomed Jesus into my heart" is akin to saying "Jesus lives in the center of my life," "I've welcomed Jesus to the deepest part of my life." It is God's life inside of us, beating at the core of who we are; the evidence of which being, a transformed life, a radical shift in priorities, a dying to self and living for God. It's a total surrender, and it's also full empowerment. As is the case with the human heart pumping blood through our body, so it is with the symbolic heart, pumping Jesus through our whole life. Should a part of our body not receive this bloodline of Jesus, it will wither and die. For sin, we desire its demise, for it to be cut off from the life-flow and for it to wither and die.

Everything comes from the heart. Values. Actions. Intent. Motives. Incentives. Comparison. The only way to live, to radically live, is to welcome God into the epicenter of our being—our heart. And such, therefore, is why behavior modification is temporal, as our action may well align back to the negative values of our heart.

God wants to transform our hearts and not just our actions. Because of this, we surrender our hearts. To abandon the high ground, the dark places, the forgotten places, the neglected places, and the secret places of our lives to the only one who can bring eternal change. By doing so, our hearts receive validation by God and become aligned to the values and priorities of the Kingdom of Heaven.

When it comes to the value placed on our lives, God is a jealous God,[61] and he is jealous of the high ground in our lives. The reason he is jealous is that he wants the best for us. As the father of two sons, I have jealousy for them. This jealousy sees my sacrifice for them, sees me provide opportunities for them, and would see me clear their path of harmful influencers. When they engage in an activity, I'm jealous for their success. When they are hurting, I'm jealous for their betterment. And this is God's jealousy. He knows our full potential, and he's jealous for us to achieve this fullness of potential. Furthermore, God is relentless in his pursuit of us, not in an odd and manipulative way, but the type of relentlessness that would see the disaster relief worker give all they have in their pursuit of the preservation of life. The relentless kind of protection and care a parent gives to their child.

---

60. Refer to Matt 22:37 NIV
61. Refer to Exod 20:5, 34:14 NIV

By saying God is jealous for the high ground in our lives is the understanding that this is the best form of living. There's perhaps a no better definition of righteous jealousy than that of a mother holding her newborn baby for the first time.

God is willing, able, and motivated to remove the clutter from the heart of our lives, done in partnership with us. He's no dictator, and quite possibly, we can see him as more passive than forceful. In a strange twist of events, the creator of the universe who lives outside of time patiently enters our time-constrained context and works at our pace. We are assured, however, that when we are ready for him, he will move. He will move with power, he will proceed with force, and he will bring transformational change. He spoke creation into being.[62] He calmed the storm.[63] He desires to create beauty in our lives and to calm our storms.

He will rid our lives of sin, just as a surgeon passionately, relentlessly, and jealously removes the disease from a person's physical body. If Jesus has come to remove our sin, we do not want to settle for second-best by trying to manage our sin by adapting behavioral change without spiritual heart transformation. We do not sin-manage, we sin-repent. We do not entertain sin. We remove ourselves from sin while remaining vigilant in reducing our exposure to sin. Not risk-management in the sense of mitigating the impact of sin; this is making real-life decisions to avoid places, circumstances, entertainment, and even people in our efforts to avoid sin.

But when sin becomes ingrained within the idols of our lives, it becomes a formidable force. Thankfully, not a formidable force in comparison to God. Instead, a formidable force that creates a dependency within the human heart. A force creating guilt and shame at the thought of the vulnerability needed to receive healing. Idol's do provide one of our most significant obstacles.

Many definitions detail what constitutes an idol in our lives. I have come to a straightforward explanation; what we give power to and what has power over us that when it is either removed or is in limited supply, we react negatively and start to covet and crave its provision or its replacement.

The idol could take on the form of mysticism, spiritualism, intellectualism, or consumerism. And my idol may be different from your idol. And an idol to one person may not necessarily be an idol to another person.

The idol occupies and consumes our thoughts, actions, and even resources. It's a power that challenges God's top place in our lives and

---

62. Refer to Ps 33: 6, 9 NIV
63. Refer to Ps 107:29, Mark 4:35–41 NIV

encourages us to remove our devotion from God and to place this devotion, attention, and focus elsewhere.

Another observable trait would be when we justify its presence in our lives:

"I know that playing football is taking all of my time and energy, and I don't even have time to read my Bible or pray, but doesn't God want me in a position of influence?"

For King Solomon, he may have said:

"having many wives might not be the best decision, but through these marriages, I'm forming alliances with kings, and this surely is good for diplomacy?"

For the CEO:

"I know there's great suffering in the world, but surely God wants us to have the best that life has to offer, after all, don't charities take care of the suffering?"

For the lazy and arrogant:

"I could help the poor, but they deserve what they get, and wasn't it Jesus who said "the poor you will always have"[64] and that it's far better to focus on Jesus?"

For those pursuing the love of money:

"I know some of this money probably comes from questionable business dealings, but I'm tithing, and this is surely more important."

For the rest of us:

"I know it's probably not the best thing to do, but it's not one of the big sins, and it's probably not causing anybody any harm."

The subtleness of most idols is in their ability to climb quietly, almost unnoticed, to the high ground and then once there, to develop deep roots that provide an anchor and to successfully tap into the flow of life running through our body. We allow the idol to live rent-free in our minds and our hearts. Often this idol will be lazy and passive but will stubbornly stay put and will react negatively to any threat that will look to dislodge it.

The cost of discipleship, therefore, becomes a reality. Having God reside in the high ground of our lives will require increasing activity on our part. It will cost the giving up of that which previously occupied the high ground. Discomfort may ensue, and a change of lifestyle and values may be needed until we are transformed into the person God desires us to be. This is why Paul refers to following Jesus as running a race.[65] It takes time, effort,

---

64. Refer to Matt 26:11

65. Refer to 1 Cor 9:24–26, Gal 5:7, Phil 3:13–14, 2 Tim 4:7–8, Heb 12:1–2 (the author of Hebrews, although not named, is often attributed to Paul) NIV

and discipline. There will be pain, and there will be discomfort, but these will pale into insignificance at the donning of the winner's crown, wherein this described race of faith, we all win.

I took up running in my mid-40s, and over the past few years, I've grown with a great appreciation for the discipline of long-distance running. The advice given for my first half marathon was the same advice given for my first full marathon: maintain your pace and don't be tempted to go fast at the start. "You can't bank time" is a universal running principle.

To reach my desired goal meant I needed to know my pace months before the race and to plan my training based on attaining this pace. On race day, maintaining my discipline and being loyal to my strategy became all-important. Finding a pacer was crucial; that one runner slightly ahead of me who exhibited signs of self-discipline to their plan, which I could trust to run at my desired pace consistently.

Running this strategy requires discipline and confidence, while many runners were heading to the first bend before me, I was confident in the start of the race and at the end of the race. A well-disciplined training regime was required, as was being around like-minded people. I train with a running group, and great relationships are formed. I'm encouraged on my performance, coached on my form, and we share a common goal and purpose. On the weekends, I train alone, and this becomes a mind-game of not giving in to the hills and not giving in to tiredness. I train on tired-legs, and this training gets me across the finish line.

Over these past few years, running has helped my posture, developed my core strength, and I've worked on my style. I'm instructed to swing my arms to maintain momentum. I'm taught to run from my core. I'm told to keep my head up, and there are many times, countless times, where every part of my body is crying out to let my head tilt forward just a little, to allow my arms to cross my chest, and not to lift my feet high enough; to let my guard down and allow poor habits in. My body is crying out for comfort and pleading with me to stop. Yet, for the long-distance, I know that I can't sacrifice my form for comfort or speed, because ultimately, comfort and speed will jeopardize my race.

Within the running club, not all runners are running the same race, and a good number of runners are there on the side-lines cheering and encouraging. The Melbourne marathon hits a grueling incline towards the end of the race, and I had two good friends run alongside me for a while, speaking encouragement into my ears; they had previous experience on the hills and knew when I would be most in need. It's hard to quantify the impact of these two runners who were there for me as I was *hitting the wall* while running uphill and maintaining pace. My coach and my support played an integral part, but ultimately, I was the only one who could run my race. And this is true for life. Only I can compete for the race set before me, yet, I have the counsel of the Holy Spirit and the provision of community to help.

The same is true for each of us. We are the only ones who can run the race set for us. We have unique missions in life, and the discipline learned through running has aided my appreciation of the work involved in fulfilling my purpose. It does take effort, though, but the reward is great. We are given all that we need to succeed, and we have an unapologetic reason to be ourselves. Many of us will spend years, perhaps even decades, not realizing our mission. We may not have complete confidence, and we can have tendencies to fall victim to our perceived deficiencies.

I read an article over the weekend of a man in his 70s. Reflecting on his life, he failed to find any semblance of meaning. Divorced, with an estranged adult child, he recalled having just one friend whom he rarely sees. He reflected on his meaningless job, and he summarised how he had made zero impact on this world, and has nothing to leave behind. He suspects that not one person will attend his funeral, and his final passing would be of no consideration. His sadness was tragic. There are many times I do doubt my worth, and I doubt my value, but these are fleeting in duration. My life has a purpose, it has meaning, and this has come through perseverance and my relationship with God, creating countless opportunities for my life to be lived in fulness.

We are created for community and compelled to spread this community for those on the outside.

Returning to the writings of Paul:

> Do you not know that in a race all the runners run, but only one gets the prize? Run in such a way as to get the prize. Everyone who competes in the games goes into strict training. They do it to get a crown that will not last, but we do it to get a crown that will last forever. Therefore I do not run like someone running aimlessly; I do not fight like a boxer beating the air. No, I strike a blow to my body and make it my slave so that after I have preached to others, I myself will not be disqualified for the prize.[66]

Our relationship with God is not dependent on works, and we are not part of a performance-based faith. Yet, we do know that we live in a fractured world, and many people are broken while trying to navigate their lives on our suffering terrestrial planet. We do know life is unkind for many people. That life is immensely cruel for many others. That life has a habit of marginalizing and victimizing the powerless. There are whole sectors

---

66. 1 Cor 9:24–27 NIV

of society who feel as though they are left behind as we look to economic theories to set a fair distribution of wealth. We need to understand pain and injustice, where it happens, how it happens, God's viewpoint, and our required response. For this reason, our faith needs to have evidence to help validate God's love to a needy world. It is for this reason that we train our bodies, and we willingly run the race for the sake of others.

We do need to prevail in our race, and we do not want to disqualify our efforts in this race; ultimately, this comes from our understanding of purpose rather than effort-based obligation.

On the other hand, slowness, apathy, and shyness will also present a cost to our transformation. When we prolong a process that could have taken months and turn this into years, we have wasted time, and the cost being missed opportunities. Another high cost is in the positioning of our lives. We turn from the self and focus on community, where the needs of the community become higher than our own needs. Perhaps this is where the rubber hits-the-road for many of us. Are we willing to count the cost of our engagement in a broken world? Are we to take on bravery in our need to challenge the powers that suppress people? This is the cost of discipleship.

Over the years, I've allowed creeping insignificance to form idol like powers over my life. I've attempted to manage this insignificance, at times, actively tendering its root systems. Roots that go deep often take time and care to remove.

Behavior modification without the transformation of the mind will not work. Jesus's freedom should be experienced through the whole of our lives, and this includes the liberating of our secrets.

34

Following Jesus is Experienced Mainly Through our Minds

"'I showed them the path to glory, but they did not follow it'" Prince Andrew continued after a short silence.

Leo Tolstoy[1]

Without any shadow of a doubt, God's love and God's redemption are perfect. There is no deficiency in God's love, and there is no battle when it comes to God's love. Love won. We are not on the winning side; we are on the victors' side. There is nothing we can do to earn this love, and there is nothing we can do to jeopardize this love.[2]

God's love is unconditional and does not require constant renewing.

However, our discovery and response to God's love are conditional. It is contingent on the renewing of the mind to be transformed into the likeness of Jesus.

We can grow apathetic towards God's love. We can become cold toward God's love. We can mute God's love and, at times, rebel against God's love, but through the darkest of our nights, we are not separated from God's love. Any sense of separation is self-imposed. There will no doubt be seasons in

---

1. Tolstoy, *War and Peace*
2. Refer to Rom 8:39 NIV

the disciple's life, mine too, where God can seem silent, yet, the hope of God remains intact, and we do not need to experience loneliness or separation.

Our experience and our response to God's love will determine our earthly lives. Whether we live with undivided hearts pursuing divine purpose or we live a life at differing levels of compromise while experiencing a divided heart.

Our battle is not against flesh and blood.[3] In many ways, it is a battle for the high ground in our lives—the battle for the mind.

The battle we face is predominantly a battle of ideas and how these ideas shape our values, self-worth, and belief. Following Jesus is lived mainly through our minds.

We have minds that need development, and we have minds designed to be renewed and transformed. Minds that can discover the reality of who we are, and minds that can accept our true identity in God. Minds that can distinguish identity from character, and differentiate between who we are and what we are. Minds that can be aligned to the perfect nature of God rather than being impacted by a flawed environment.

The unnamed author of the Epistle to the Hebrews wrote:

> This is the covenant I will make with them after that time, says the Lord. I will put my laws in their hearts, and I will write them on their minds.[4]

God would trust us, and God would validate us to such a degree that he willingly and voluntarily writes his laws on our minds. Matthew Henry's Commentary[5] suggests this is accomplished through the work of the Holy Spirit pouring wisdom, will, and power into our minds.

Through Jesus and the Holy Spirit, God has provided the keys to this perfected living. Without the mind of God, this could not be achieved. Perfection, then, remains both in a state of being and the promise of becoming.

The potential of the human mind, when aligned to the perfection of God, really would know no limits. It does not make us equal with God, but it does show the level of validation that God places on our lives. To live with renewed and transformed minds is one of the greatest achievements we can attain, while the downgrading of our minds through poor self-perception is one of the greatest tragedies we do face. It is perhaps not too hard to realize that the costliest battles for many of us, are the battles that take place in our minds. Every despicable act known to humanity is birthed from the

---

3. Refer to Eph 6:12 NIV
4. Heb 10:16 NIV
5. Henry, Commentary on Hebrews 10:16

mind, where a combination of thoughts paves the way for ideas to become organized into plans, leading to action and ultimately a consequence.

Consider how much suffering has been dealt to millions of victims over the years resulting from plans forged in the depths of dark minds.

In his letter to Titus, the Apostle Paul twice urges the need for taking ownership and responsibility for our thought life:

> They are to be the boss over their own desires.[6]

And,

> He must be able to think well and do all things in the right way.
> He must live a holy life and be the boss over his own desires.[7]

Our faith is not passive, nor does it require the handing over of our minds to an external force. The follower of Jesus is called to the highest of thought life. To take on the full responsibility of the mind. To discover and investigate, while engaging on behalf of a world in need. Our intellectual capacity has much depth, and our creative ability has such breadth. We can make the right decisions based on empathy and compassion while aligning to the mind of Christ for the pursuit of life-defining and life-transforming decisions.

For many, the gap between the devil's rhetoric and the resulting flawed environment, and the promise of freedom in God can seem vast. In reality, however, to bridge this divide is the simplest of human effort. It's the acknowledgment of the need for God and the confession of our life without God:

- We can live as a victim, or we can live as one favored by God[8]
- We can live as a no-one, or we can live a life of greatness
- We can live with the grief of having no-worth, or we can believe that we are worthy
- We can live with the separation of feeling we do not deserve love, or we can live in the knowledge of being loved by the God who is love
- We can become the person of our insecurity or we can become the person God dreams of

We can choose to live in a self-imposed echo chamber where the negative beliefs and harmful opinions we hold as being true, become reinforced

---

6. Titus 2:2 NLV
7. Titus 1:8 NLV
8. Refer to Matt 5:3 AMP

as they reverberate through a negative self-assessment of our lives. In this instance, we build barriers that impede our ability to discover liberation in Jesus. Alternatively, we can voluntarily enter into the louder echo chamber of a flawed society where the beliefs and opinions that society holds as being true are relative and non-consistent.

Humans do need validation, and humans do need the sense of our lives being on track and having a purpose. Previously, we identified God as the one who validates our lives as being very good, and the one who welcomes each of our lives unreservedly with eternal love. This validation brings the sureness that we humans need. We discover the fullness of our identity and the meaning of life in the never-changing person of Jesus.

Without knowledge of Jesus, we search for validation, and this search will take place within an ever-changing society, where societal values are non-constant, and opinions change. This environment can agitate our need for belonging and validation through the illusion of shifting ideas and changing value-systems. Satan will actively look for ways to amplify these messages transmitted, and he'll identify ways for these messages to reverberate through our minds, generating thoughts and ideas, while leading to actions and ultimate consequence.

I've spent many nights outside the Gatwick Hotel with people for one reason, or another have fallen through society's cracks. Before its conversion, The Gatwick Hotel ominously carried the title as Australia's "most infamous rooming house,"[9] regarded by many as "hell hotel"[10] and a "house of horrors."[11] It was known as a place where you can be murdered in your room, robbed, bashed, or offered drugs; yet, it also provided shelter for some of Melbourne's most needy, neglected, and vulnerable citizens. We would take hot food and hot drinks, yet hunger was not the overriding reason people came to our soup-van. They came because we listened and cared. They came because they could share their story and open up their lives. They had someone who would listen to them without any judgment. For a few hours each Thursday evening, they were known, they were seen, and they were valued. Their lives experienced a sense of validation.

The corner where we set-up was not a pretty sight and most of the general public would cross the road to avoid walking through the dozens of people assembled. I admit on a different night, on a different corner, I would do the same as the sight was confronting, yet it was an environment where,

---

9. Sutton, *Hell hotel*
10. Sutton, *Hell hotel*
11. Sutton, *Hell hotel*

on occasion, I would take my family. We provided community and a safe place for a few hours each week.

In some ways, society has failed the people who relied on the Gatwick Hotel. In other ways, their lifestyle choices had led to negative consequences. In many ways, illness and relational breakdown had led to their dependency on food hand-outs and social housing. However, their greatest need remained; to be known, to be seen and to know they are cared for by the only one who can bring liberation and validation.

One of our brightest beacons of human hope was found in the humble life of an Albanian nun, affectionately known as Mother Teresa. Mother Teresa not only cared for those who others wouldn't care for, but she also spoke with a wisdom that reflected her closeness to the heart of God:

> Loneliness and the feeling of being unwanted is the most terrible poverty.[12]

Humans crave unconditional love, and we will search until we find it; either intentionally realizing this pursuit, or unintentionally searching and becoming victims of unfulfilled expectations.

A challenge remains whereby sin can become so ingrained in society and culture, and whereby sin can become deeply lodged in our psychological makeover that we can fail to recognize sin. Similarly, we can downplay the seriousness of sin, and refer to these decisions as individual choices in modern living. Sin is described as *missing the mark* or described as failure, or error. It takes great strength to admit failure. It takes humility to step away from this pride of not wanting to own up to our mistakes.

Not to say society, by definition, is corrupt and wrong. Society is actually at the heart of God's plan for humanity. He called us to be a community, and we need community, and differing levels of good is found in communities around the world. But any community that does not acknowledge the Lordship of Christ will have cracks in its foundation, and as these cracks widen, structural damage becomes a reality, and people can fall through the cracks.

Jesus became so we become, and by doing so, Jesus established a radical model for society. A recalibration of society. At the heart of the human is the desire for a relationship with God. Our hearts have a magnetic north pointing to God and pointing to the in-built call from the depths of our being for freedom. Freedom is a birthright secured with the death and resurrection of Jesus.

We spend our lives in search of God, many times, without realizing it.

12. Teresa, Goodreads

We look for belonging.
We look for acceptance.
We look for an intimate relationship.
We look for love.
We look for purpose.

We fear decay.
We fear isolation.
We fear rejection.

These are hallmarks of our spiritual yearning. Every human is on a spiritual journey seeking God. Some realizing, some searching but without the language and discernment to describe and comprehend the essence of their search. We are all in need of a spiritual reset in our lives—a spiritual transformation that brings purpose and meaning to our lives, and liberation and freedom.

"Every man that knocks at the door of a brothel is looking for God."[13] At the heart of this confronting statement attributed to G. K. Chesterton, is the description of a human soul looking for love, but looking in the wrong place, and causing immense damage while on their search. Consider the rise of relationship-based reality television shows and the constant popularity of romantic comedies. We are created for relationship, ultimately with God but also each other, as companions on this hard road of life. Since collectively leaving Eden, we do face toil, sweat, and pain, and we now have to work hard to provide an income and to face the pain of bringing forth family. Attempting this life in isolation is untenable.

People will search in the wrong places for love, but ultimately, they are searching for a connection with God and with others. We are created for perfect intimacy, and God is the only one who can heal the emotional pain and wounds that come through seeking perfect intimacy in the framework of an imperfect society.

The fundamental basis of this search repeats in all of our lives; in different ways. The search will look different, but the underlying need is the same, our need for God and our need for intimacy, connection, and depth of belonging that only God can provide. This side of heaven, we will only experience shades of this perfect community, but we have the hope that not only keeps us going through the often-dark night of the soul, but we also have the responsibility to point others to this hope.

---

13. This quote, being attributed to Chesterton, is not conclusive although being referenced in numbers of places

Jesus came to point towards God's perfect and unconditional love and the awesome display of his grace. Jesus didn't come to judge. Instead, he came to be judged. There are many accusations against God; that he is not fair and that he is judgmental. In some ways, this is true. Jesus didn't come to judge; he came to be judged. Judged by us, and condemned to receive capital punishment. We accuse God of being judgmental when in actuality, it is us who judged God. We've grown reliant on the self-defense mechanism of shift-blaming, starting with Adam and Eve, perfected through the years, used against Jesus, and countless times since.

Simply put, it was not fair that Jesus had to die for us and it was not fair that he was judged on our behalf, yet, by doing so, he lifted the guilt from our hearts and made the way to live perfected lives through his once, and for always, forgiving of our sin and the removal of our guilt.

Our task, as discovered in the Great Commission,[14] is to point others to identify with God's love so they too can find liberation. We do this at the individual person-to-person level, where the commission included in the Gospel of Mark[15] is a call to a specific generation at one particular time; if we miss the opportunity to reach this particular generation, the opportunity does not repeat. And we do this through the generations as commissioned in the Gospel of Matthew,[16] taking a long-term view of how society functions. This multi-generational commission commits the follower of Jesus to engage with the people within society as well as the structural framework of society itself.

I have many friends who come from, and who have fled governmental systems of control, be it based on religion or be it based on philosophy. This has led me to consider different forms of government and structures of society. Every type of government will disappoint its citizens to one degree or another. Still, it's my observations, that governments aiming to control thought life will ultimately fail.

Mind control is beyond any governments realm of authority, and the government's intent to restrict freedom often leaves them inept at providing answers, from the scream of mass suffering to the silent cry of the broken-hearted.

The Kingdom of God can only provide these answers, and the work of the follower of Jesus is to make known these answers to societies in need. Humans are designed for freedom, and we will rebel at any attempt to remove this freedom. The availability of the Tree of the Knowledge of Good

---

14. Refer to Matt 28:16–20, Mark 16:15–18 NIV
15. Refer to Mark 16:15–18 NIV
16. Refer to Matt 28:16–20 NIV

and Evil[17] remains one of the most debated aspects of the Bible; yet, it is a vivid demonstration of the value God places on freedom of choice. It's as a birthright and inheritance from a loving God who valued freedom at any cost, and any form of government that attempts to compromise this God-given inheritance will be fighting an unwinnable fight. I value a society whose citizens are freely able to disagree with my faith, but where a Government resists the calls to sanction the ideas generated through my faith.

The truth be known; this remains a struggle.

The devil prowls like a raging lion[18] and remains successful at identifying and exposing flaws in our lives. He'll exploit these flaws to gain an advantage. He'll poke around in our lives, in our history, in our perceived failures and our low self-esteem, our low self-value and low self-worth, and tempt us with "joyless grabs for happiness."[19] He'll deliberately elevate simply to aggravate our flaws and cause division. He'll actively be engaged in the process of seeking personal glory and the donning of crowns, and of the individual needing validation on a growing consistency, and of seeking accolade as a foundation of identity; or, advocating that we incorporate fear into our character to establish a perceived sense of insecurity. Whereas the devil will look to on-load such things, Jesus will offload these areas and will replace them with the fruit of the spirit[20] and the gifts of the spirit.[21] We trade-in the old-self and are given the new-self.[22]

Jesus has done all that is needed. We now need to do our part and to take the next step; surrender to him. Let go of the protective boundaries that keep us in our perceived illusionary state of comfort.

The question remains one of readiness and willingness:

- To get over self-centeredness
- To walk free from self-entitlement and reject self-obsessiveness
- To step over an offense, and to stop our unhealthy reliance on excuses and blame-shifting
- To acknowledge the disruptive nature of self-entitlement
- To acknowledge that seeking forgiveness for those seemingly small errors is essential to the lifestyle Jesus has called us to

17. Refer to Gen 2:9 NIV
18. Refer to 1 Pet 5:8 NIV
19. Gal 5:19–21 MSG
20. Refer to Gal 5:22–23 NIV
21. Refer to 1 Cor 12: 8–11 NIV
22. Refer to Eph 4:22–24 NIV

FOLLOWING JESUS IS EXPERIENCED MAINLY THROUGH OUR MINDS

God does not ignore our flaws. Instead, he pays the ultimate price to bring healing to our flaws. He'll actively redeem our faults, and use our flaws for his glory. An open wound will leave a scar when healed, and this scar can be redeemed into a testimony of God's goodness in contrast to our pain.

God's work in our life is faultless. Satan has no authority or ability to touch God in our life; it is when we remove God from areas of our lives that Satan gains influence. The challenge we face is continuously allowing God to enter every area of our lives, to surrender our high ground, the dark mysteries, the hurts, the secret life, the pain, and the fears about our future. The more of God, the less selfish ambition and vain conceit.

Let the Holy Spirit be the gatekeeper to our mind and our soul.

This battle, raging around us, originates from tension[23]—the tension between good and evil, right and wrong, and our interpretations and accommodation of such. The Bible remains clear concerning the internal conflict that exists between the transformational work of the Holy Spirit in our lives and the desires of our sinful nature.[24] Salvation brings freedom, yet, our response to freedom is what defines the level of salvation we experience through this spiritual conflict. We are set free from the law, yet, we do not have a license to use this freedom in the any-such way we choose and to expect immunity from the consequences of our actions; nor, are our freedoms to be self-centered.

The freedom won on our behalf obliges us to consider others before our own needs.[25] Many may see this not as freedom but rather as slavery. In God's kingdom, however, our freedom validates and empowers our obligation to the community. We need renewing and regenerating constantly, and we need to be alert to the schemes of our enemy. True freedom is found in surrender. Jesus steers us away from the penalty of sin, and the Holy Spirit guides us away from the temptation to sin.

This battle does not dislodge God or impede God. It does, however, impact our lives, causing division that negatively impacts relationships and societies.

Any division is a wound in the human experience. It's a negative spiritual reality influencing the mind to engage in acts of division. A spiritual answer is required for this spiritual problem. Every action Jesus took was a deliberate act against physical and spiritual division. This counter-cultural, almost rebellious lifestyle cost Jesus his life. Yet, in his death, we have been given our freedom and the perfect example of how to live.

---

23. Refer to Matt 26:41, Gal 5:16–18 NIV
24. Refer to Matt 26:41, Gal 5:16–18 NIV
25. Refer to Phil 2: 1–18 NIV

Live unoffended but be offended at slavery.
Live at peace yet disturb the oppressor.
Seek reconciliation rather than isolation.
Take a stand but not by squashing others.
Be purpose-driven yet not glory-seeking.

Realize that valuing our identity is one of the most significant forms of rebellion we can take in the face of a billion-dollar economy feeding off peoples' need for validation and approval.

Focus on others, become vulnerable, deny our wants, and heartfully and joyfully engage with life. Division only takes away from society. It can never add.

I consider God values each of us equally. Yet, in saying this, God may allow for levels of discomfort in our body to turn us toward him. I consider these to be God-nudges. In such nudges, God is more the describer of pain rather than the prescriber of pain, where through the Bible, God is seen describing the frightful consequence of poor decision making. The prescriber of our suffering stems from our rebellion at Eden, whereas God is the prescriber of healing and redemption. God's mercy redeems our past, and, when we allow, he'll use the testimony of our history to liberate not just ours but others' futures.

Jesus provides all the confidence we will need through his name.

35

Confidence in the Name of Jesus

O, Lord have mercy on ye! poor crittur. Han't ye never heard of Jesus Christ?" "Jesus Christ,—who's he?" "Why, he's the Lord," said Tom. "I think I've hearn tell o' the Lord, and the judgment and torment. I've heard o' that." "But didn't anybody ever tell you of the Lord Jesus, that loved us poor sinners, and died for us?

HARRIET BEECHER STOWE[1]

THERE ARE SOME OCCASIONS in the Bible where God provides a person with a new name:

- Abram became Abraham[2]
- Sarai became Sarah[3]
- Jacob became Israel[4]
- Simon became Peter[5]

---

1. Stowe, *Uncle Tom's Cabin*
2. Refer to Gen 17:5 NIV
3. Refer to Gen 17:15 NIV
4. Refer to Gen 32:28 NIV
5. Refer to John 1:42 NIV

- Saul to Paul[6]

These new names would generally be associated with defining the individual's purpose while establishing their new identity, or names given to reveal God's plans. Names are important. My birth name is Nicholas, and my current name is Nicholas. My parents chose my name, Nicholas, and this is the name that God uses when defining me.

My name does not need to change as I have inherited the name above all names, the name of Jesus. This name now resides in my life and has become the foundation on which my identity rests.

"We are in Christ"[7] is a profound statement repeated through the New Testament. There is no higher authority, and there is no higher name than that which is already mine. By choosing to live in me, Jesus has perfected my identity. Instead of a new name, I'm called a friend of God,[8] with the Holy Spirit's empowerment within.

Our perfected identity is based on a name rather than appearance, our education, or other forms that can be easily compared and contrasted. The name of Jesus is above all names,[9] and at this name, knees will bow, and this provides us with the completeness of confidence. We do not need to strive. We do not need to work. We do not need to worry. In one sense, Jesus has provided humanity with a level playing field, where we share the same foundation of our identity. Our identity is perfected by him who chose to reside in our lives.

When we attempt to build our confidence in anything besides the name of Jesus, we will experience an incompleteness that negatively impacts our confidence. In trying to develop confidence in physical appearance, in our financial standing, our societal positioning, or our education, family, sports, our intellect, or the number of social media followers, these will all require constant validation. Maintaining validation through anything other than God will take energy and resources; it will become relentless and non-achievable. Receiving God's validation simply requires faith, rest, and relationship.

There does exist a gap between our current state of affairs and the perfected identity available through Jesus. To bridge this gap will require the

---

6. God as the author of this new name is not recorded; instead, it is more likely that Saul (referencing his Hebraic background) and Paul (Latin; referencing his Father's Roman citizenship) were interchangeable names

7. Refer to Rom 8:10, 2 Cor 4:6–7, 2 Cor 13:5, Gal 1:15–16, Gal 2:20, Gal 4:19, Eph 3:17, Col 1:27, 2 Thess 1:10

8. Refer to John 15:15 NIV

9. Refer to Phil 2:9 NIV

constant renewing and transformation of the mind through the empowering of the Holy Spirit, combined with the discipleship that requires us to count the cost of being a follower of Jesus. Bridging this gap requires that we make Jesus Lord in all areas of our lives. In one sense, we do not make Jesus Lord, as Jesus already carries the title of Lord,[10] all we can do is recognize Jesus as Lord in our own personal and particular circumstances, and to then allow Jesus to be the Lord of our lives.

Through rejecting the spiritual, we become blinded to the source of freedom.

Before our liberation, we were captives, bound in the chains of bondage.[11] To the average person on the street, this statement may seem ludicrous. After all, and for most of us, there are no physical chains, no prison gates, and there are no detention centers. Yet, how many would consider the spiritual resemblance of chains, gates and detention residing in our lives. And to be free of these spiritual bondages will take a God-empowered resilience and defiance.

---

10. Refer to Phil 2:11, Rev 17:14 NIV
11. Refer to Rom 6:17–19, Gal 5:1 NIV

36

Practicing the Greatest Act of Defiance

To clasp the hands in prayer is the beginning of an uprising against the disorder of the world.

KARL BARTH[1]

MY HOPE IN WRITING this book is to encourage further consideration of the importance and uniqueness of life; mainly, the strength of our identity. We are not the sum total of our behavior. Each of us is loved and deeply cherished by God. God, who continues to call us *very good*. God loves us, and for the follower of Jesus, our identity is perfected through Jesus.

The basis of this book is the credible hypothesis that, as followers of Jesus, we take on the status of being perfectly imperfect, and this is the key to successful living. God is perfect, and we are flawed; yet, God in us makes us flawesome. Unfortunately, this does not necessarily lead to a comfortable life.

We will continue to experience pain in the physical, and we will continue to experience pain in the emotional. The difference for the follower of Jesus, however, is how our pain can be redeemed to become purposeful. If nothing else, it reiterates our need of a healer, humbles our heart, and opens the door to our desperate need for help.

The quicker we can come to terms with not possessing the inherent ability to fix our broken world, and to fix our tender minds without the power and intervention of Jesus, life will start to make more sense.

1. Russell, *Overcoming Evil God's Way*

Despite the claim that we have perfected identities, we can remain ransomed to our flawed character. Within this tension, the Holy Spirit is active. Active in bringing more profound levels of liberation to our character. We do not, and we cannot hide from the reality of living our lives within an imperfect world; yet, we have already been perfected through Jesus while continuing the process of being perfected through the ongoing work of the Holy Spirit. Perfected identity and the continuing perfecting of our character marks our time on this earth.

Our character often becomes the window to our lives, and we are generally judged through character rather than identity and defined by character instead of identity. And this is where a contradiction exists. Nonetheless, a contrite heart and speedy and sincere response to our wrongdoings, through the seeking of forgiveness and the movement towards reconciliation, will allow the testimony of Jesus to shine through the cracks of our lives.

There does remain the danger of considering we are what we are, rather than being who we are. And we can then stay at differing levels of bondage to this flawed thinking, considering that we are of low-worth. Alternatively, to think that we are of high worth, higher than our humility can regulate.

This apparent contradiction is the journey of discipleship, and this journey does take time, and it's normal for it to take time.

However, we are, each of us, on a unique journey, and God's work in our lives is tailor-made to meet our peculiar needs. For some, there may be a rapid and elevated change in lifestyle, whereas, for others, we do seem to progress gradually. Yet progress, we must, and progress, we do.

We have established that our identity is found in a name, and this name is Jesus. And this is how God defines us and validates us, who we are rather than what we are. Satan will look to deconstruct this truth and to nullify our real value by declaring that we are indeed the product of our flawed behavior and our flawed character.

Systems of the world may then strengthen this definition and successfully manipulate us to consider what we need; alternatively, to become fearful or greedy of what we lack while offering an array of marketeers and solutions to provide a temporary fix. We often will then comply with this definition, and succumb to this manipulation, and oblige by taking on the role of a consumer of all that will inhibit life.

A toxic mix can result where we define ourselves by a combination of all three: identity, character, and need—resulting in three competing voices speaking three possible narratives. God's narrative of life. Our narrative sustaining existence, and Satan's narrative promoting death; albeit, this narrative will most likely appear as a pleasurable temptation rather than death. Yet, an attraction that quickly leads to spiritual decline.

We then identified and discussed the importance of validation in our lives, a word that brings dread and fear to many. Consider the teacher being validated in the classroom, or the validation of the resumé representing the hopeful candidate. Yet, validation is for our good, and indeed, we do crave validation, knowing that how we are living and what we are doing is purposeful and has meaning. God initiated validation, and therefore set the precedent for all future validation. He validated us at the very beginning of time as being *very good*, and this validation is in line with the philosophy of bringing *life and life to its fullest*. There also exists validation that generates judgment and comparison: two conditions that humans are ill-equipped to handle.

We further discussed the process of renewing our minds and the transformation of our lives. A spiritual process that can and needs to become a daily practice. It's argued that we make upwards of 35,000 conscious decisions each day.[2] Thirty-five thousand opportunities to practice the discipline of bringing our lives in alignment with the values and principles of God.

The renewing of the mind is a human responsibility, and this is integral to the discipleship process. Despite it being a human responsibility, it remains impossible to complete without the work of the Holy Spirit in our lives, combined with the ongoing process of welcoming Jesus to the high ground of our lives. Requiring the dislodging and removal of idols, we have embraced, and idols with the tendency to claim our high ground. It is through discipleship that we die to self and make Jesus Lord.

We discussed life as a journey. We are on a journey. A journey of discovering the fullness of God and a journey deeper into the kingdom of God. A kingdom void of deficiency. And when the lack is eradicated, temptation has no appeal. One day we will experience God in fullness. Until that day, we will remain tempted to alleviate these feelings of deficiency with consumables, wealth, position, experience, and people. In doing so, we elevate these above God, often unwillingly, but still, voluntary.

Within God's kingdom, there is no class system, no disadvantage, no favored status, no discrimination, and we will never be downtrodden. Nor is there lack, nor deficiency. No temptation can rival what we have, nor rival the fullness of what is ours to come. Lure has no hold when, in comparison to what we possess, temptation does not work. It no longer has appeal.

And, within the kingdom of God, we are seen, we are known, and we are loved. Flowing from this will come purpose, meaning, and passion.

In this age of being liberated while still waiting for full freedom, Satan will agitate, highlight, and promote our flaws. He will tempt us to turn

2. Graff, *How Many Daily Decisions*

certain flaws into crowns, the flaw of pride, the flaw of self-sufficiency, and the flaw of perfectionism. He will actively help us to transform what is a passion to become a platform of personal glory.

However, God purchased our flaws at Calvary, and he will heal and redeem these flaws to bring life and life in its fullness. Humans desire to be seen, and we all want to be known, and we all search for the same thing—a relationship with God.

Our identity is as a beloved child of the King.

Yet, how many would attest to feeling imprisoned despite the lack of physical bars? Of being abused with no apparent way out? Of seeing only darkness as we consider our future? Of the need to cut the skin just to feel alive from the flow of blood? To feel as though we are in a tightening vice? Of being manipulated and downtrodden? Of crippling debt? Of unending pain? Of no way out? And so forth.

While it may be true that there is no physical infrastructure keeping us bound, the unseen reality does remain.

The Bible describes Satan as the enemy of the human race and all that God loves.[3] Satan, as:

- the one who attacks our character[4]
- the wicked one[5]
- the ruler of this world[6]
- the god of this age[7]
- the prince of the power of the air[8]
- the tempter;[9] and,
- our accuser[10]
- while deceivingly appearing as "an angel of light"[11]

---

3. Refer to Rom 8:37-39, Eph 6:10-11, Col 1:13-14, 2 Thess 3:3, Jas 4:7, 1 Pet 5:8-9 NIV
4. Refer to Job 1:9-11 NIV
5. Refer to Matt 13:19, 38 NIV
6. Refer to John 12:31 NIV
7. Refer to 2 Cor 4:4 NIV
8. Refer to Eph 2:2 KJV
9. Refer to 1 Thess 3:5 NIV
10. Refer to Rev 12:10 NIV
11. 2 Cor 11:14 NIV

Satan is the one who comes to kill, steal, and destroy.[12] Who, when he speaks, he speaks his native tongue, and this native tongue being lies.[13]

One reading of the history of our world is summarised as God sharing authority with us. Much non-conclusive writing and discussion are generated on the theory of Adam relinquishing his God-given authority to Satan. Nonetheless, we do know that Satan has a form of influence that is empowered through the actions and desires of humans; and that he will use this influence to destroy. A review of the Bible finds evidence of Satan carrying titles signifying some form of power.[14]

And, we can interpret the book of Revelation to provide a well-researched conclusion that at some point in the timeline of our fallen world, Satan is empowered to bring destruction; seemingly without the crucial element of human involvement.

Be it an independent and autonomous power with authority to kill, steal and destroy, or whether this power is in Satan's ability to influence humans to carry out his acts through manipulating human thought, is another discussion. What we can be sure of, however, is the evidence before us; hatred, greed, pain, genocide, war, and prejudice. Broken lives and fractured communities living and competing in a deteriorating world.

The story of Jesus's victory on the cross is one of defeating and disempowering Satan while returning authority to humans.[15] Resulting from this victory, we have become empowered, and Satan is disempowered, yet we can inadvertently and unwillingly share this power with the forces of evil. We do this every time we doubt our identity and look to something other than God to alleviate our loneliness and to achieve our need for intimacy. Or, when we consider the right to fulfill self-centered satisfaction at the expense of the needs of another.

The devil will look for the opportunities to create chaos for us, and to then capitalize on this chaos by engaging us with the practice of blame-shifting while advocating we succumb to imposter syndrome, and ultimately to turn hearts away from God.

Either the chaos of our broken world; war, famine, disaster; where the deep philosophical questions build accusations against God "if there is a God, why does he allow suffering," or "if there is a God, why didn't he just stop this or that from happening." Or the more hidden and subtle chaos of our inner lives, anxiety, fear, and greed. The success of Satan can be in

---

12. Refer to John 10:10 NIV
13. Refer to John 8:44 NIV
14. Refer to Eph 6:12 NIV
15. Refer to Matt 28:18-19 NIV

each of us, thinking we are the only ones going through a particular pain; alternatively, the crippling fear of shame will stop us from reaching out for help. From civil war to divorce, Satan stirs up the chaos.

Some of this chaos will become global events.

As I'm typing, I'm keeping updated on the unprecedented chaos brought by COVID-19 as it continues its relentless rampage through the fabric of society, infecting millions and killing hundreds of thousands, decimating healthcare systems, and triggering economic recessions. This chaos has come through a virus; yet, inequality, poor governance, the differing values we place on human life, and global politics can dictate our response to this chaos. And these responses can mean a life saved or a life lost, a society reconstructed with haste, or a society facing years of further disruption generated from decimated economies and infrastructure.

More personalized chaos can seem to pitch its tent within the framework of our mind. Thus, creating a trigger point for future agitation. We do well to understand these triggers in general terms, but also specific terms.

When we engage in activities and situations that will cause these triggers to be activated, we are wise to avoid them. Avoiding bars for the recovering alcoholic, and avoiding night clubs for the times we make poor relational choices. Not subscribing to the full array of available television channels as we have previously struggled with restricted adult content. And avoiding the toxic relationships that lead us to gossip, accusation, and slander.

Or, when these activities and situations are unavoidable, we need to position ourselves not to be negatively impacted; or at least to minimize this impact.

Comparison is one of the most significant contributors to the uncertainty that can quickly evolve to bring chaos in our lives. Comparing ourselves with others can be akin to investing in future insecurity.

It need not be this way, however.

Would you join the most significant movement, the greatest act of defiance to a system set against us by opening the palms of your hand and simply pray while being ready to act?

Ready to end the pursuit of the temporal, to reject the marketeer of forbidden fruit, to turn from a system of greed, to register protest against the objectification of the human body. And believe in the same power that raised Jesus from the grave?

An act of defiance that is the foundation of intimate relationship with the creator of the universe who calls us friend and who values us; the one in whom we are seen, we are known, and we are loved.

The greatest act of defiance found in the simplest of expression; arms slightly extended, palms in an upright cup-shaped position. Uttering the words "Come, Lord Jesus, Come."[16] Come into my life. You are welcome. Come into my mind. You are welcome. Come into my worries. You are welcome. Come into my dreams. You are welcome. Transform my life through the renewing of my mind.

Come, Lord Jesus, Come.

All this is possible. If we simply surrender—surrendering our flawed lives in exchange for liberation. To realize our identity is perfected through Jesus. All the while, our character goes through the process of transformation. Living well within our temporal human body is a gift. We only need to accept it.

To accept the beauty of living imperfectly perfect: the fatally flawed becoming confidently flawesome, through the love of the one who is Awesome.

---

16. Based on Rev 22:20 NIV

Also Available from the Author

The Nine Veils: The Reputation of God & Our Struggle for Identity. Eugene, Oregon: Wipf & Stock

The Nine Veils explores the link between reputation and identity, making the case that if we desire to have the fullness of identity, we need to have a clear view of God, an unveiled view.

It's working title became "30,000 Sunrises," referring to the number of days demographers expect me to live. The number of days I have to determine the meaning and purpose of life, to develop a healthy understanding of God's character, and overcome the obstacles that stand in the way.

I explore the values of two opposing kingdoms; the Kingdom of God bringing life and life to the full and the failed kingdom of the devil who will take every opportunity to kill, steal, and destroy.

The devil aims to destroy God's reputation and to crush our identity, achieved when we wear spiritual-veils, veils that block and obscure God and hinder our relationship.

We often develop a wrong understanding of God through doubt: either we doubt all that God says he is, or we doubt he can meet our unique circumstances. When doubt robs our freedom, we can develop a fear-based perspective and interpret our relationship with God as one of reaching targets and maintaining performance. Alternatively, we personalize God to such a degree that, often subconsciously, we expect him to meet our entitlements.

The book identifies nine spiritual-veils that people wear, nine veils distorting our view and damaging our identity.

1. Absent-God veil
2. Performance-God veil

3. Karma-God veil
4. War-God veil
5. Angry-God veil
6. Schizophrenic-God veil
7. Happy-God veil
8. Genie-God veil
9. Safe-God veil

Through my own journey and walking alongside many others, I consider that each of us can relate, in some way, to the concept of these veils. Through testimony, I use real-life stories to amplify this area; stories of intimacy and vulnerability.

Be it the result of doubt, fear, or entitlement, our understanding of the ways of God, of God's character and his love, becomes tainted. We may still see evidence of light, but we've lost the ability to determine the position of God, and we form our assumptions of God based on misinformation. Over time, the gap between our assumptions and the real character of God widens as we attempt to navigate this confusing void.

The book does not ignore the tough questions of life as they represent our need for identity:

- Who am I?
- Where am I from?
- Why am I here?

Or, how they represent our uncertainty of God's reputation:

- Why does God allow?
- Why is there suffering?
- Why doesn't God stop?

These critical questions directly influence our understanding of God's reputation and our identity.

While some of the harder questions of faith, as they relate to God's reputation, are also explored:

- The Conquest of Canaan
- The Revelation narrative

Yet, these are not discussed from in-depth theological perspectives. Instead, they are addressed in the context of God's good character; of a God who is gracious and compassionate, slow to anger and rich in love.

The reader is invited to consider their questions and concerns, and even accusations that they may have against God. Central to the philosophy of this book is God's comfort in being asked questions. Yet, the way we ask questions becomes essential, as a son or daughter deeply loved by God, or as an accuser.

God is further explored through providing three sure anchors in our knowledge of God's character (God's Exodus 34:6 autobiography, the person of Jesus, and the priorities of the Holy Spirit). These three anchors become a solid foundation in helping to navigate a society that can reject God and even resent God.

The book ends with a challenge to live veil-free. To use our confidence in God to reach a hurting world, a world desperately needing to meet the God who loves them and where the battle for personal identity and the need for confidence in God's reputation is of paramount importance in the twenty-first century.

www.nineveils.com
Facebook: The Nine Veils
Instagram: nine_veils

Reader Reviews

This a deep-dive into the big questions we all ask. Matthews probes some of the most perplexing questions in theology and the quest for self-understanding

—Dr. Allan Demond
(Author, Lecturer & Snr Pastor, NewHope)

I hadn't intended to look through it this quickly but found it fascinating and insightful. I like the concept of the veils and your overall theological emphasis in this work

—Aaron Simms (Author, Pastor, Publisher)

It's truly a must-read book.

—Billy Hallowell (Director of communications and content, PureFlix.com Author, "The Armageddon Code," "Fault Line," and "Left Standing")

An excellent book. He grapples with lots of different issues about God's nature and character as well as who we are. I would highly recommend this book

—Steve Goode (Author, International Director Mercy Ministries International)

The author suggests that our view of God is sometimes obscured by the lens of doubt, fear or entitlement causing us to think of God as angry, judgmental, or silent, which in turn distorts our view of ourselves

—Chowdene Community Church

Brilliant and brave

—Reviewer

This unique book makes the case that if we desire to have the fullness of identity, we need to have a clear view of God. An unveiled view

—Reviewer

The author is brave and passionate about this subject. Difficult subjects are tackled well, and it is easy to read and clearly explained. Its strength is its simplicity

—Reviewer

Your writing shows great maturity born from an in-depth study of God's word and living among God's struggling people. Please keep writing

—Reviewer

Having just finished reading Matthews thought provoking book, I found that the book challenged my view of God and also who I am in Him. It's an eye-opener and really making me think. The book is well worth a read

—Reviewer

I just started the book, and I find it so interesting that I spend more time mulling things over in my mind and talking to God about it

—Reviewer

It's gutsy yet easy to read

—Reviewer

I read your book, and I am about to read it again. It has opened doors of understanding for me. The issue of identity today has become extremely significant

—Reviewer

This is a well researched and well-written book. Humans have many ideas about God, most of them are in error. Nicholas looks at the incorrect beliefs we follow that keep us from seeing God accurately. He calls them veils

—Reviewer

Exceptional, challenging, and inspirational book!
I can see myself on every page

—Reviewer

Very thought-provoking book which is well worth a read—leaves the reader with much to think about

—Reviewer

Tremendous and impactful. It really helps to understand the impact of identity

—Reviewer

Great book, I found the thoughts, ideas, and revelations impactful, which has greatly enriched my spiritual life and relationship with God

—Reviewer

Amazing book! Such a key issue. Well written & thought-provoking, containing surprises I hadn't thought of or considered!

—Reviewer

I can confidently state your work was found to be a thought-provoking read,
tackling issues of great importance and sensitivity,
and conveying a positive message

—Reviewer

Reading the chapter on the Suffering God—an eye-opener.
Really making me think

—Reviewer

This read is definitely an interesting one to say the least

—Reviewer

Very thought-provoking
—Reviewer

Bibliography

Ahlquist, Dale. 2003. *G. K. Chesterton: The Apostle of Common Sense*. San Fransisco: Ignatius.
Alderson, Heather. n.d. *God Wants Each One of Us . . . Empty Handed*. Self-published.
Anderson, Annelise & Martin. 2009. *Reagan's Secret War: The Untold Story of His Fight to Save the World from Nuclear Disaster*. New York: Crown, Kindle Edition.
Augustine, St. n.d. Goodreads. Accessed 07 15, 2020. https://www.goodreads.com/quotes/6390550-this-is-the-very-perfection-of-a-man-to-find).
Brontë, Charlotte. 1847. *Jane Eyre*. England: Smith, Elder & Co.
Chambers, Oswald. 1924. *My Utmost for His Highest*. Dodd, Mead & Co.
———. 1935. *The Psychology of Redemption (Making All Things New)*. Crewe: Oswald Chambers Publications.
Collazo, Julie Schwietert & Rogak, Lisa. 2013. *Pope Francis in His Own Words*. New World Library.
Crabb, Dr Larry. 2009. *66 Love Letters: A Conversation with God That Invites You into His Story*. Tenessee: Thomas Nelson.
Dostoyevsky, Fyodor. n.d. Goodreads. Accessed July 15, 2020. https://www.goodreads.com/quotes/126038-every-ant-knows-the-formula-of-its-ant-hill-every-bee.
Du Bois, William Edward Burghardt. n.d. Goodreads. Accessed July 15, 2020. https://www.goodreads.com/quotes/7335951-when-you-have-mastered-numbers-you-will-in-fact-no.
———. n.d. Goodreads. Accessed July 15, 2020. https://www.goodreads.com/quotes/7335951-when-you-have-mastered-numbers-you-will-in-fact-no.
———. n.d. National Public Radio. Accessed July 15, 2020. https://www.npr.org/2011/02/09/133623714/honoring-leading-thinker-w-e-b-dubois.
Du Bois, William Edward Burghardt. 1987. "Strivings of the Negro People." The Atlantic.
e-artnow, Kindle edition. 2017. *Henry David Thoreau—The Man, The Philosopher & The Trailblazer*.
Einstein, Albert. 1955. "Old Man's Advice to Youth: 'Never Lose a Holy Curiosity.'" *LIFE Magazine* 64.

Graff, Frank. n.d. "How Many Daily Decisions Do We Make?" Accessed July 15, 2020. http://science.unctv.org/content/reportersblog/choices#:~:text=Researchers%20at%20Cornell%20University%20estimate,each%20day%20on%20food%20alone.&text=It's%20estimated%20that%20the%20average,are%20both%20good%20and%20bad.
Gumbel, Nicky. 2019. *Bible in One Year: A Commentary*. London: Hodder & Stoughton.
Hammond, Lily Hardy. 1916. *In the Garden of Delight*. New York: Thomas Y. Crowell Company.
Henry, Matthew. n.d. *Matthew Henry Commentary on the Whole Bible (Complete)*.
Hourly History. 2016. *Greek Mythology: A Concise Guide to Ancient Gods, Heroes, Beliefs and Myths of Greek Mythology*. Hourly History.
Hugo, Victor. 1887. *Les Misérables*. Translated by Isabel F. Hapgood. New York: Thomas Y. Crowell.
Johnson, Boris. 2020. "There is such a thing as society, says Boris Johnson from bunker." *The Guardian*, 30 March.
Johnston, Alan. n.d. "Libya 1911: How an Italian Pilot Began the Air War Era." Accessed July 15, 2020. https://www.bbc.com/news/world-europe-13294524.
Josephus, Flavius. n.d. *The Works of Flavius Josephus*. Translated by William Whiston, AM, London. As viewed on Google Books.
Keller, Timothy. 2009. *Counterfeit Gods: The Empty Promises of Money, Sex, and Power, and the Only Hope that Matters*. London: Hodder and Stoughton.
Krockow, Eva. 2018. "How Many Decisions Do We Make Each Day? The Number of Choices is Hard to Estimate, but it's Higher than you'd Expect." 27 September. Accessed July 15, 2020. https://www.psychologytoday.com/au/blog/stretching-theory/201809/how-many-decisions-do-we-make-each-day.
Kushner, Harold, S. 2002. *When Bad Things Happen to Good People*. London: Pan Books.
Lewis, C., S. 1952. Mere Christianity. London: HarperCollins.
———. first published 1958. *Reflections on the Psalms*. Harcourt Brace.
Mahoney, Daniel J. 2001. *Aleksandr Solzhenitsyn: The Ascent from Ideology*. Lanham, Maryland: Rowman & Littlefield.
Mandela, Nelson. n.d. Goodreads. Accessed July 15, 2020. https://www.goodreads.com/quotes/278812-as-i-walked-out-the-door-toward-the-gate-that).
Manning, Brennan. 2005. *The Ragamuffin Gospel*. Colorado Springs: Multnomah.
Matthews, Nicholas. 2018. *The Nine Veils: The Reputation of God & Our Struggle for Identity*. Eugene, Oregon: Wipf & Stock.
Netland, Harold A. 2015. *Christianity and Religious Diversity: Clarifying Christian Commitments in a Globalizing Age*. Grand Rapids, MI: Baker Academic.
Noble, T. A. 2013. *Holy Trinity: Holy People: The Theology of Christian Perfecting*. Eugene, Oregon: Cascade.
Orwell, George. 1937. *The Road to Wigan Pier*. Maplewood.
Patton, George Smith. n.d. Goodreads. Accessed July 15, 2020. https://www.goodreads.com/quotes/895096-if-everyone-is-thinking-alike-then-somebody-isn-t-thinking.
Rand, Ayn. 1936. *We the Living*. London: Macmillan.
Roosevelt, Franklin Delano. 1938. *Public Papers of the Presidents of the United States: F.D. Roosevelt: Volume 7, 1938*. Random House.
Russell, Stephen. 2008. *Overcoming Evil God's Way: The Biblical and Historical Case for Nonresistance*. Guys Mill: Faith Builders Resource Group.

Sanders, J. Oswald. 1958. *A Spiritual Clinic: Problems of Christian Discipleship*. Chicago: The Moody Bible Institute.

Sheldon, Charles Monroe. 1897. *In His Steps*. Chicago Advance.

Spurgeon, Charles Haddon. 2013. *The Complete Works of C. H. Spurgeon: Volume 15: Sermons 848 to 907*. U.S.A.: Delmarva.

St. Paul's Cathedral. n.d. "St. Paul's Cathedral." *The Light of the World Decoded. A Resource Book for Teachers and Students*. https://www.stpauls.co.uk/documents/Education/Light%20of%20the%20world%20booklet.pdf.

Stowe, Harriet Beecher. 1852. *Uncle Tom's Cabin*. Boston: John P. Jewett.

Sutton, Candace. 2018. "Hell Hotel: Real Story of The Block's New Site." *news.com.au*, 3 August.

Swan, Laura. 2007. *The Benedictine Tradition: Spirituality in History*. Edited by Laura & Zagano, Phyllis Swan. Minnesota: Liturgical Press.

Teresa, Mother. n.d. Accessed July 12, 2020. https://www.catholic.org/clife/teresa/quotes.php).

———. n.d. Goodreads. Accessed July 15, 2020. https://www.goodreads.com/quotes/224828-loneliness-and-the-feeling-of-being-unwanted-is-the-most.

The Lausanne Covenant. n.d. "The Lausanne Covenant: Point 4 The Nature of Evangelism." Accessed July 15, 2020. https://www.lausanne.org/content/covenant/lausanne-covenant#cov).

The Voice Bible. 2012. *Commentary of Genesis 1:29–31*. Nashville: Thomas Nelson.

Thomas, William Isaac. n.d. *Oxford Reference*. Accessed July 15, 2020. https://www.oxfordreference.com/view/10.1093/oi/authority.20110803104247382.

Thompson, Geoff. 2019. "ABC Religion & Ethics." 19 December. Accessed July 15, 2020. https://www.abc.net.au/religion/christmas-and-christianity-proximity-to-power/11824134.

Tolstoy, Leo. 1894. *The Kingdom of God is Within You: Christianity Not as a Mystic Religion But as a New Theory of Life*. Translated by Constance Garnett. New York: The Cassell Publishing Co.

———. 1942. *War and Peace*. Translated by Louise and Aylmer Maude. New York: Simon and Schuster.

Tutu, Desmond Mpilo. 2011. *God is Not a Christian*. San Fransisco, California: HarperOne.

Women's Own. 1987. "Interview with Margaret Thatcher."

Yancey, Philip. 1995. *The Jesus I Never Knew*. Grand Rapids, MI: Zondervan.

Zechariah, Chafee. 1919. "Freedom of Speech in War Time." *Harvard Law Review* 932–73.

www.ingramcontent.com/pod-product-compliance
Lightning Source LLC
Chambersburg PA
CBHW071439150426
43191CB00008B/1181